THE BREAD
MACHINE BIBLE

THE BREAD MACHINE BIBLE

MORE THAN 100 RECIPES FOR
DELICIOUS HOME BAKING WITH YOUR BREAD MACHINE

ANNE SHEASBY

DUNCAN BAIRD PUBLISHERS

LONDON

THE BREAD MACHINE BIBLE
Anne Sheasby

Distributed in the USA and Canada by
Sterling Publishing Co., Inc.
387 Park Avenue South
New York, NY 10016-8810

This edition first published in the UK and USA in 2009
by Duncan Baird Publishers Ltd
Sixth Floor, Castle House
75–76 Wells Street
London W1T 3QH

Copyright © Duncan Baird Publishers 2009
Text copyright © Anne Sheasby 2009
Photography copyright © Duncan Baird Publishers 2009

The right of Anne Sheasby to be identified as the
Author of this text has been asserted in accordance
with the Copyright, Designs and Patents Act of 1988.

All rights reserved. No part of this book may be repro-
duced in any form or by any electronic or mechanical
means, including information storage and retrieval
systems, without permission in writingfrom the
publisher, except by a reviewer who may quote brief
passages in a review.

Managing Editor: Sarah Epton
Managing Designer: Manisha Patel
Designer: Saliesh Patel
Commissioned Photography: William Lingwood

10 9 8 7 6 5 4 3 2

Library of Congress Cataloging-in-Publication Data

Sheasby, Anne.
  The bread machine bible : more than 100 recipes for
delicious home baking with your bread machine / Anne
Sheasby. -- 1st ed.
     p. cm.
  Includes bibliographical references and index.
  ISBN 978-1-84483-795-3 (alk. paper)
  1. Bread. 2. Automatic bread machines. I. Title.
  TX769.S398785 2009
  641.8'15--dc22

                                                2008039098

Typeset in DIN and Univers
Color reproduction by Colourscan, Singapore
Printed in Malaysia for Imago

For information about custom editions, special sales,
premium and corporate purchases, please contact
Sterling Special Sales Department at 800-805-5489 or
specialsales@sterlingpub.com.

Publisher's note: While every care has been taken
in compiling the recipes for this book, Duncan Baird
Publishers, or any other persons who have been
involved in working on this publication, cannot accept
responsibility for any errors or omissions, inadvertent
or not, that may be found in the recipes or text, nor for
any problems that may arise as a result of preparing
one of these recipes. If you are pregnant or breast-
feeding or have any special dietary requirements or
medical conditions, it is advisable to consult a medical
professional before following any of the recipes
contained in this book.

a note about the recipes

All spoon and cup measures are level unless otherwise
stated. All flours should be measured by scooping the flour
into a cup measure and leveling the surface. Large eggs
should be used in the recipes, unless specified otherwise.

We have included baking temperatures for electric and
gas ovens. Remember if you have a fan-assisted oven you
need to reduce the oven temperature slightly and/or adjust
the cooking times. Please refer to the owner's manual for
more specific information.

Please note that bread machines vary, so add the
ingredients to the bread pan in the order specified in your
owner's manual (if this differs from the directions given in
these recipes). The order in which we recommend you add
the ingredients to your bread pan will be applicable to many,
but not all, bread machines, so please make sure you read
and follow your owner's manual carefully before preparing
any of these recipes. All the recipes in this book have been
tested using a Panasonic bread machine.

contents

bread over the centuries

Bread has been part of the staple diet of many countries worldwide for thousands of years and it is still held in high esteem within many cultures. Bread forms an important part of our everyday diet, providing a good, basic food that is both nutritious and delicious.

In centuries gone by, bread was initially baked over open fires, but gradually traditional ovens of brick or stone were built into homes and bakeries. Such ovens are still in use in the more rural areas of countries around the world, but the advance of technology and the development of modern ovens has seen the traditional types much less used. Over time, an increasing range of breads has been created, and new ingredients and flavorings have been incorporated in basic recipes. Today, we have a vast range of delicious loaves available to us in all shapes and sizes, offering many different tastes and textures.

Bakers, grocers, delicatessens, farmers' markets, and supermarkets stock an array of traditional loaves, as well as popular regional loaves and breads from around the world. We can choose from sweet or savory breads, some plain, others flavored with ingredients such as seeds, olives, cheese, herbs, sun-dried tomatoes, spices, or fruit. Increasing ranges of organic and specialist breads, such as gluten-free or dairy-free breads, are also readily available, and artisan bakers offer traditional loaves as well as creating new and interesting breads.

Nevertheless, it's difficult to beat the rich aroma and full flavor of freshly made homebaked loaves, and making your own bread can be simple and very rewarding, especially with the use of a bread machine. These increasingly popular appliances are ideal for those of us with little time to spare, providing the satisfaction of baking your own bread using fresh, nourishing ingredients.

our daily bread

Bread is an appetizing food as well as being nutritious, and we should try to include a good proportion of starchy foods, such as bread, in our everyday diet. Many basic breads are low in fat, and bread provides an excellent source of starch—the more complex carbohydrate that provides your body with a sustained energy source—as well as some protein. All breads provide dietary fiber, and whole wheat and whole grain varieties contain nearly four times more than white loaves, in addition to lots of B vitamins and some iron. American law requires all flours that have had wheatgerm removed during milling to have added niacin, riboflavin, thiamin, and iron. Some millers also add vitamins A and D.

Obviously, some of the more elaborate enriched breads and doughs contain more calories and fat than basic loaves, but these, too, can be enjoyed as special-occasion breads or treats within a balanced diet. Many of the quick bread recipes also provide healthy snacks.

bread machine recipes for all types of bread

This book by no means includes all bread machine recipes, but it offers many different types of breads from all over the world, enabling you to create delicious breads in your own home at a fraction of the cost of commercially produced loaves.

We include the basics of breadmaking and bread machines, essential information on key ingredients and techniques, as well as some useful hints and tips. Each recipe chapter is filled with a tempting selection of recipes, ranging from simple, rustic everyday breads to enriched, specialty loaves, and from traditional flat breads to quick-and-easy quick breads, loaf cakes, and baked goods. We also include a section on gluten-free breads for those with a sensitivity to gluten.

Each recipe is clearly written and easy to follow, and includes guidance tips, such as preparation and baking times, as well as the number of servings.

By mastering your bread machine, and using the recipes in this book as a guide, you can experiment with all kinds of flavors, shapes, and textures to suit your own tastes. So, we invite you to take a leisurely journey through this eclectic collection and hope you will enjoy the experience of creating and baking your own bread at home for many months and years to come.

ingredients for breadmaking

Bread has four essential ingredients: flour, yeast, liquid, and salt. Other ingredients, such as sugar, fat, and eggs, can be added to produce different types of bread.

Flour

Types of flour

For traditional yeasted breads made in a bread machine, choose bread flour. It is available in several varieties, the most common being white and whole wheat. All-purpose and bread flours are both made from hard wheat, but bread flour has a higher gluten content, which stretches the dough and traps in air as it bakes, producing a well-shaped loaf with a good rise and a light, open texture. Flours vary between brands, but choose organic, unbleached bread flour, if possible.

All-purpose or self-rising flours are ideal to use in quick breads (although some yeasted doughs, such as French Bread, use a mixture of flours). Quick breads tend to have a closer, more crumbly texture.

Breads made with hard whole wheat flour tend to be slightly denser and coarser in texture than white breads, but are flavorful and nutritious. For a lighter-textured loaf, you can use half white bread or all-purpose flour and half whole wheat bread flour. Mixed-grain flour produces a lighter brown loaf with a nutty flavor. Stoneground whole wheat flour is ground between stones, hence the name, and this gives the flour a slightly roasted, nutty flavor.

Other flours, such as barley, millet, and spelt flours, have a low gluten content, but can be combined with bread or all-purpose flours to make delicious loaves. Rye flour, which has a good gluten content, often produces dough that is sticky and difficult to handle, so it is frequently mixed with other flours to make it more manageable.

Gluten-free flours

If you have an intolerance of or sensitivity to gluten, you will need to avoid flours that contain gluten. Because gluten is the protein that strengthens and binds dough in baking, you might need to find alternative binding agents when using gluten-free flours. A combination of starches often works better than a single type, and adding ingredients, such as egg, grated apple, or mashed banana, can also help. It should be noted gluten-free flours tend to make dense loaves with a close texture, and they tend to absorb more liquid than ordinary flours, so you might need to add extra liquid to dough mixtures if you are adapting standard recipes into gluten-free ones. A selection of gluten-free white and whole wheat flours is available from supermarkets, health food stores, and mail-order sources, especially websites.

Alternatively, you can combine a selection of naturally gluten-free flours, such as rice flour, gram (chickpea) flour, buckwheat flour, cornmeal or maize meal flour, tapioca flour, and potato flour. Gluten-free bread mixes are also available from health food stores and mail-order sources, and many of these are suitable for use in a bread machine.

It is important to remember when making bread by hand or using a bread machine that all utensils should be washed thoroughly before and after use, as even the slightest trace of wheat can cause an allergic reaction in someone who suffers with celiac disease or who has an intolerance to wheat.

Yeast

Yeast is an essential ingredient in breadmaking as it causes the bread to rise. It is a living organism that feeds on the sugar and later the starches in the flour and it then releases a gas (carbon dioxide) that makes dough rise. Yeast is available in several different forms including fresh compressed yeast, traditional active dry yeast, and instant dry yeast (also called rapid rising).

For this cookbook, in all relevant recipes, we have used instant dry yeast. This type of yeast is recommended for use in a bread machine and it is simple and convenient to use. Fresh compressed yeast and traditional active dry yeast (granules) are not suitable for use in a bread machine.

Instant dry yeast

Instant dry yeast is a combination of dry yeast and the bread improver ascorbic acid (vitamin C), which accelerates the action of the yeast during the fermentation process. It is available in handy ¼-ounce packages, or it can be bought in 4-ounce jars, which need to be kept in the refrigerator once opened. Bread machine yeast, produced by some manufacturers specifically for using in bread machines, is another form of instant dry yeast and they can be used interchangeably. Yeast won't work if it is stale, so always follow the package directions for storage and adhere to the best-before date on the package.

Other leavening ingredients

While yeast is the most common leavening ingredient used in breadmaking, other raising agents, such as baking powder and baking soda, are also used for making some quick breads in a bread machine.

Liquids

The liquid used in breadmaking is usually water, although milk or a mixture of milk and water is used in some recipes. Other liquids, such as plain yogurt or eggs, can also be used in some bread machine doughs. One main difference between making bread by hand and making bread in a bread machine is the temperature of the water or liquid used. Whereas warm water or liquid is used when making bread by hand, cold water or cool milk (at room temperature) is usually required for bread machine recipes (check your bread machine manual for specific guidance on this)—unless using the "Rapid Bake" or "Fast Bake" program, when warm water (or other liquid) might be required. If the timer-delay facility is being used, fresh milk should be replaced with dried skim milk powder and water, and eggs and other highly perishable ingredients should not be used.

Salt

Salt improves the flavor of bread and it also helps the dough to rise in a controlled and even way, resulting in a well-risen, even loaf. However, salt also slows down the action of yeast, so follow the quantities given and be careful not to add too much if you're adapting your own recipes.

Sugar and other sweeteners

Sugar helps to feed the yeast and make it more active, hence, encouraging fermentation to take place more quickly, but too much sugar can impede the effectiveness of yeast. Modern types of yeast, including instant dry yeast, no longer need sugar as the flour provides them with enough food, but for good measure it is usual to add a little sugar in bread machine recipes.

White, soft light brown, and soft dark brown sugars can all be used in bread machine recipes, and in some recipes honey, golden syrup or light corn syrup, maple syrup, malt extract, and molasses are used to add flavor and colour. Artificial sweeteners are not suitable for breadmaking.

Fats

Some bread machine recipes include a little fat, such as butter. Others can require the addition of oil or melted butter. Fats add flavor and richness, as well as improving the keeping qualities of the bread, but too much fat will slow down the action of the yeast. We have specified using butter in most of the recipes (where applicable), but in many cases you can use margarine or a similar alternative fat, if preferred. Low-fat spreads are not recommended for use in a bread machine.

Bread mixes

There is a good range of bread mixes available, many of which are suitable for use in a bread machine, and they are ideal for creating delicious breads with little fuss. They include white, whole wheat, mixed-grain, and seed bread mixes, as well as flavored varieties. Gluten-free bread mixes are also available.

Simply follow the directions given on the package and also refer to your owner's manual for more advice. Check the weight of the ingredients in the package does not exceed the total amount your bread machine can handle, and check the consistency of the dough after 5 minutes: add a little extra liquid if the mixture seems too dry.

Bread mixes are best baked immediately, rather than using a timer-delay facility, as you cannot separate the yeast from the liquid.

breadmaking techniques

Please note the following information is applicable only if you are using the "Dough" program on your bread machine. It does not apply to loaves that are made and baked completely in a bread machine.

Punching down and proofing the dough

If you are using the "Dough" program on your bread machine, once this program finishes, the dough should be removed from the bread pan and "punched down." This process smooths out any large air pockets and insures an even texture in the bread. To punch down the dough, turn it out onto a lightly floured surface, then punch the risen dough with your fist to deflate it and knock out the air. Knead it briefly—only 2 to 3 minutes—to redistribute the yeast and the gases formed by fermentation. Sometimes, at this stage, other ingredients, such as olives, chopped herbs, chopped sun-dried tomatoes, chopped nuts, seeds, or dried fruit, can be kneaded into the dough (if they have not already been added during the "Dough" cycle).

The dough is then shaped or molded as required, covered, and left in a warm place until it doubles in size. This is known as the proofing stage. It is important not to overproof the dough, otherwise the bread can collapse during baking—make sure the dough rises only until it doubles in size. If it does not rise enough at this stage, however, the loaf will be dense and flat. To test if the dough has risen enough, simply press it lightly with your fingertip. It should feel springy and the indentation made by your finger should slowly spring back and fill.

For professional-looking bread, proofing baskets (which are often used by professional bakers) can be used for proofing the dough. Proofing baskets are wicker baskets lined with linen or canvas, which are lightly floured, and they provide extra support to the bread dough during its final rising. They are available in round or long (baguette) shapes from good kitchenware stores and online cookware suppliers. Once the dough has risen in a basket, you simply turn it out onto a floured cookie sheet and bake as normal.

Shaping bread

If you are using the "Dough" program on your bread machine, once this program finishes and you punch down the dough, it can be shaped by hand in various ways. Common shapes include large rounds or ovals, braids, and batons. Dough can be formed into rolls of varying sizes and shapes, including rounds, knots, long rolls, and rings. Dough can also be slashed with a sharp knife in various ways before or after proofing: slash the top of the loaf along its length; make crisscross lines over the top of the loaf; cut a deep cross over the middle, or cut several diagonal slashes across the top of the loaf.

Slashing the tops of loaves is done not only for visual effect but also for practical reasons, to provide escape routes for the air and to control the direction and extent of the rise during baking. The earlier you slash the dough, the wider the splits in the baked loaf; and the deeper the slashes, the more the bread will open during baking. Use a sharp knife and a swift, smooth action when slashing the dough, to avoid tearing it.

Glazing bread

If you are using the "Dough" program on your bread machine, once the program finishes and you punch down and shape the dough, brushing a loaf with a glaze before baking enhances the color of the baked bread, as well as adding flavor to the crust. Glazes not only help to give the loaf an attractive finish, but they also add moisture by producing steam that helps to expand the loaf and insure even baking. Additionally, glazes help toppings, garnishes, or decorations to stick to the surface of the dough.

Breads can be glazed before (sometimes during) or just after baking. The most common ingredients used to glaze loaves are water, milk, or beaten egg, but you can also try melted butter, olive oil, light cream, warm honey, sugar syrup, or a thin frosting for a variety of different finishes.

Finishing touches for bread

Once the dough has been shaped and glazed, but before it is baked, various ingredients can be used for topping or finishing the bread, and each ingredient creates a different effect. Try sprinkling loaves or rolls with seeds, cracked or kibbled wheat, rolled oats, salt flakes, grated cheese, or fresh herbs before baking, or dust with a little flour. For sweet breads, try dusting with confectioners' sugar or sprinkling with sugar, chopped nuts, slivered almonds, dried fruits, or grated chocolate, usually after baking.

Some enriched or specialty doughs might need covering to prevent them browning too much during baking. If the bread shows signs of browning too quickly, simply cover it loosely with foil toward the end of the baking time.

storing bread

Most homemade bread is best when served freshly baked and on the day it is made, and it should be eaten within 1 to 2 days, because it becomes stale quickly. Bread made from enriched doughs, with a high fat or sugar content, is also best eaten when freshly baked, but will keep up to 3 days.

Bread is best stored in a cool, dry, well-ventilated bread bin or an earthenware bread crock, but not in the refrigerator. The cold draws moisture out of the loaf, making it dry and stale. Wrap bread in foil or a plastic food bag if it has a soft crust, and in a paper or fabric bag if it is crusty.

Bread also freezes well for a short time—up to about 1 month. Simply seal the bread in a plastic freezer bag, or alternatively cut the loaf in half or into slices and freeze in convenient portions, ideal for thawing when required. Unwrap and thaw frozen breads at room temperature.

Quick and yeast-free breads tend to become stale quickly and these are often best eaten freshly baked or within 1 to 2 days. Many store-bought breads contain preservatives or flour improvers, hence, they have a longer storage life than homemade breads.

bread machines

There is a wide range of bread machines to choose from, and selecting a model to suit you will depend on several factors, including size or capacity required and budget. Do some research before buying a bread machine to make sure you get the most suitable model for your needs.

Bread machines save time and effort and they are relatively simple to use. Before you begin, it is worth familiarizing yourself with your machine and experimenting with the different programs and options. Make a few basic bread recipes from the owner's manual before you try any new recipes. Practice makes perfect, and you will soon master how to use and program your machine, and then be ready to experiment.

The names of the programs used, such as "Rapid Bake" or "Basic White," may also differ slightly from one model to another. The delay-timer facility is useful for when you are not at home or are asleep—coming home or waking up to the smell of freshly baked bread is truly wonderful!

Programs vary between models, but many include a "Basic White" or "Normal;" "Whole Wheat;" "Multigrain;" "Rapid Bake" or "Fast Bake;" "Sweet," "Raisin Bake," or "Raisin Beep;" "Dough;""Raisin Dough;" and "Bake Only" programs. Some models also include more specialized programs, such as "French," "Cake," "Sandwich," "Pizza," and "Jam." Refer to your owner's manual for more details of the programs included in your bread machine.

Some bread machines also offer a choice of three crust colors: light, medium, or dark. If your machine does not have this option or you prefer a darker crust, however, once the loaf is baked, simply brush the top of the baked loaf with a little melted butter, or egg yolk mixed with water, and brown under a hot broiler or in a preheated oven at 400°F 5 to 10 minutes.

Bread machine pans vary in size between models, and on large models you might have the option of making up to three different sizes of loaf. We have selected a medium-size loaf for these recipes (where relevant), which should suit most bread machines.

We have given ingredient quantities and cooking instructions for each recipe in this book, but it is very important you read through your owner's manual before embarking on any of the recipes. Bread machines vary, so you might find, for example, you have to add the ingredients to the bread pan in a slightly different order from that given in a recipe. Simply add the ingredients to the bread pan in the order specified in the manual.

Useful tips when using a bread machine

- Take the bread pan out of the machine before adding the ingredients. This helps to avoids spillage in the bread machine body.

- Accurate measuring is probably the most crucial factor for a successful loaf when using a bread machine. Always use a proper set of measuring cups and spoons. Many models include a measuring spoon and cup for liquids, so use these if they are provided.

- It is important that the salt, sugar, and yeast are kept separate from each other in the bread pan until mixing commences. This is less important if you are making some breads using the "Rapid Bake" or "Fast Bake" program, as the ingredients are mixed as soon as the program begins.

- Keep the yeast dry and separate from any liquids added to the bread pan until mixing commences. Separate the yeast from the liquid by adding the yeast before or after the flour (according to your owner's manual)—the flour acts as a temporary barrier between the yeast and liquid.

- Once the initial mixing cycle begins, if you are able to, it is worth briefly lifting the lid and scraping down the sides of the bread pan with a flexible plastic or rubber spatula for even mixing, in case some of the ingredients stick to the corners of the bread pan.

- Once your bread machine is in rising or baking mode, resist the temptation to open the lid, as the cold air interferes with the temperature inside the machine and can slow down the process. Some models incorporate a viewing window so you can check on your bread's progress.

- When using the "Raisin Bake" or "Raisin Beep" program, add extra ingredients and flavorings when the machine makes an audible sound or beep. Check that all the ingredients are mixed in and use a flexible plastic or rubber spatula to scrape down the sides of the bread pan, if necessary. If you do not have this facility on your machine, add the extra ingredients about 5 minutes before the end of the kneading cycle.

- If you are using the "Dough" program, when this program finishes and you have punched down and shaped the dough, the shaped loaf or rolls should be placed on either a greased or a floured cookie sheet(s) (or other pan) before baking. Some enriched or specialty breads are best baked on a greased, rather than a floured, cookie sheet to avoid sticking. With each recipe, we include guidelines on preparing the bread pan, cookie sheets, or other pans, where applicable.

- In some recipes, we use the "Bake Only" program, which is ideal for "baking" recipes, such as quick breads, loaf cakes, and so on. Many bread machines include this program but some don't, so choose these recipes only if your bread machine includes this facility.

- When using the "Bake Only" program, such as when making quick breads or loaf cakes, remove the kneading blade or paddle, if possible, from the bread pan before use. Grease and line the bottom of the bread pan with nonstick baking paper or waxed paper before adding the quick bread or loaf cake batter. With some machines, the kneading blade is fixed and cannot be removed.

- When using the "Bake Only" program, remove the bread pan from the machine before transferring the quick bread or loaf cake batter to the pan. Then place the bread pan back in position in the bread machine before closing the lid and proceeding with the baking process.

- When using the "Bake Only" program, set the timer, if possible, to the minimum time recommended in the recipe, or according to the timings suggested in the owner's manual. Check the loaf after the shortest recommended time—and before the timer finishes, if necessary—and remove the baked loaf if it is ready. With some bread machines, you can set the timer for as long as you wish (within reason), while on others the timer is preset to a specific amount of time. With some bread machines this preset time can be reset immediately once the initial baking time finishes (if the recipe needs additional baking time, for example), while with other models the timer cannot be reset straightaway, so bear this in mind when choosing recipes to make in your particular bread machine. Your owner's manual should give you more advice about this.

- Even if you don't use the timer-delay facility on your bread machine, the timer itself will be invaluable when you are making bread, so you can see how many minutes are left to run on the program.

- Don't touch the outside of the bread machine during the baking cycle, as it can sometimes get very hot and might cause burns if you are not careful.

- Once the bread is baked, always take the bread pan out of the machine using oven mitts.

Gluten-free breads

When making gluten-free breads in a bread machine, it is important to refer to the owner's manual for guidance on the specific programs recommended. The "Rapid Bake" or "Fast Bake" program usually produces the best results.

Bread machine recipes—troubleshooting

Results can occasionally be disappointing when making bread in a bread machine and it is useful to know what might have gone wrong. Most, if not all, bread machines include a troubleshooting guide that details common errors, including problems with loaf size and shape, bread texture, and crust colour and thickness, as well as bread-pan problems and operational errors. Please refer to your owner's manual for more details.

adapting recipes for use in a bread machine

There is no easy formula for adapting conventional recipes for the bread machine, but the best advice is to look through the recipes in this book to find one similar to a favorite conventional recipe and use it as a rough guide. It is also worth checking the owner's manual as this might give advice for adapting your own recipes to suit that particular model. Once you have tried a few recipes in your bread machine, you will soon get the feel for how to adapt your own recipes.

Useful tips for adapting your own recipes

- First, make sure you use the correct quantities for the bread machine, insuring the total quantity of ingredients will fit into your bread pan. Do not exceed the recommended maximum. If necessary, reduce the flour and liquid quantities to match the quantities in a similar recipe.

- Use the flour and water quantities given in the recipes in this book as a guide and always refer to the owner's manual before starting a recipe. Keep the flour and liquid in the correct proportions. You might find you need to add a little more water than the amount given in handmade recipes, but this will vary depending on several factors such as the type of recipe itself, other ingredients used, and so on. With a bit of practice, you will soon get the feel for approximately how much liquid to add to different basic quantities of flour.

- Always replace fresh compressed yeast and traditional active dry yeast (granules) with an appropriate amount of instant dry yeast. (For more details refer to the owner's manual.) As a rough guide for whole wheat bread, use 1 teaspoon instant dry yeast for up to $2\frac{2}{3}$ cups flour or $1\frac{1}{2}$ teaspoons instant dry yeast for up to $4\frac{2}{3}$ cups flour.

- If the timer-delay facility is being used, fresh milk should be replaced with dried skim milk powder and water, while eggs and other highly perishable ingredients should not be used.

- If your conventional recipe uses egg, include the egg as part of the total liquid measurement.

- Check the consistency of the dough during the first few minutes of mixing. Remember bread machines require a slightly softer dough than handmade recipes, so you might need to add a little extra liquid. The dough should be wet enough to relax back gradually. If the dough is crumbly or the machine seems to be laboring, add a little extra water. If the dough is sticking to the sides of the pan and doesn't form a ball, add a little extra flour.

CHAPTER 1

basic & everyday breads

In this chapter you will find a selection of delicious breads that are ideal for regular baking. We include basic loaves, cobbs, and braids, as well as a collection of slightly more unusual flavored breads that are enjoyed all over the world, many on a daily basis.

Choose from rustic, homely bread recipes such as Garden Herb Bread, Honey-Oatmeal Bread, Cottage Loaf, Milk Loaf, and Flowerpot Breads. Or, try authentic recipes from farther afield, such as French Bread, Pesto Whirl Bread, or Greek Black Olive Bread, as well as Herby Polenta Bread, Caraway Seed Bread, or Garlic Bubble Ring.

basic white bread (pictured left)

PREPARATION TIME 10 MINUTES   **COOKING TIME** VARIES ACCORDING TO BREAD MACHINE

MAKES 1 LOAF (SERVES 10)

1½ cups water
3½ cups white bread flour
1 tablespoon skim milk powder
1½ teaspoons salt

2 teaspoons sugar
2 tablespoons butter, diced
1 teaspoon instant dry yeast

1 Pour the water into the bread pan. Sprinkle the flour over, covering the water completely. Sprinkle the milk powder over the flour. Place the salt, sugar, and butter in separate corners of the pan. Make a small indent in the middle of the flour and add the yeast.

2 Close the lid and set the machine to "Basic White"/"Normal" (or equivalent), then select the loaf size and crust type. Press Start.

3 After baking, remove the bread pan from the machine and turn the loaf out onto a wire rack to cool. Serve in slices.

basic brown bread

PREPARATION TIME 10 MINUTES   **COOKING TIME** VARIES ACCORDING TO BREAD MACHINE

MAKES 1 LOAF (SERVES 10)

1½ cups water
heaped 1¾ cups whole wheat bread flour
1¾ cups white bread flour
1 tablespoon skim milk powder

1½ teaspoons salt
2 teaspoons sugar
2 tablespoons butter, diced
1 teaspoon instant dry yeast

1 Pour the water into the bread pan. Sprinkle each type of flour over in turn, covering the water completely. Sprinkle the milk powder over the flour. Place the salt, sugar, and butter in separate corners of the pan. Make a small indent in the middle of the flour and add the yeast.

2 Close the lid and set the machine to "Basic White"/"Normal" or "Whole Wheat" (or equivalent), then select the loaf size and crust type. Press Start.

3 After baking, remove the bread pan from the machine and turn the loaf out onto a wire rack to cool. Serve in slices.

cottage loaf

PREPARATION TIME 20 MINUTES, PLUS MIXING & KNEADING TIME IN BREAD MACHINE, PLUS RISING & RESTING
COOKING TIME 30 TO 35 MINUTES   **MAKES** 1 LOAF (SERVES 10 TO 12)

1¼ cups plus 2 tablespoons warm water
   (or according to bread-mix package directions)
1 package (1 lb. 2 oz.) white bread mix

1 teaspoon salt
all-purpose flour for dusting

1   Pour the water into the bread pan. (For a good-shaped cottage loaf, the dough needs to be firm enough for the bottom circle of dough to support the top piece without sagging, so you might not need to add all the water.) Sprinkle the bread mix over, covering the water completely. Close the lid, set the machine to "Dough," and press Start.

2   Meanwhile, grease or flour 2 cookie sheets and set aside. When the dough is ready, remove it from the machine and punch it down on a lightly floured surface, then cut off one-third of the dough. Shape into plump balls and place each one on a cookie sheet. Cover and leave to rise in a warm place until double in size.

3   Preheat the oven to 425°F. Gently flatten the balls of dough and carefully place the smaller ball on top of the larger one. Push the floured handle of a wooden spoon down through the middle of the dough to join the 2 pieces together, then slightly enlarge the hole with your fingers. Leave the loaf to rest 5 to 10 minutes.

4   Dissolve the salt in 1 tablespoon hot water, then lightly brush over the loaf and dust with a little flour. Using a sharp knife, make slashes around the top and bottom of the loaf.

5   Bake 30 to 35 minutes, or until the bread is golden brown and sounds hollow when tapped underneath. Transfer to a wire rack to cool. Serve in slices.

homestyle whole wheat bread (pictured right)

PREPARATION TIME 10 MINUTES   **COOKING TIME** VARIES ACCORDING TO BREAD MACHINE
MAKES 1 LOAF (SERVES 10)

1½ cups water
3 cups whole wheat bread flour
heaped ¾ cup white bread flour
1½ teaspoons salt

2 teaspoons sugar
2 tablespoons butter, diced
1 teaspoon instant dry yeast

1 Pour the water into the bread pan. Sprinkle each type of flour over in turn, covering the water completely. Place the salt, sugar, and butter in separate corners of the pan. Make a small indent in the middle of the flour and add the yeast.

2 Close the lid and set the machine to "Whole Wheat" or "Multigrain" (or equivalent), then select the loaf size and crust type. Press Start.

3 After baking, remove the bread pan from the machine and turn the loaf out onto a wire rack to cool. Serve in slices.

farmhouse loaf

PREPARATION TIME 10 MINUTES   **COOKING TIME** VARIES ACCORDING TO BREAD MACHINE
MAKES 1 LOAF (SERVES 10)

1½ cups water
2¾ cups plus 2 tablespoons white bread flour,
    plus extra for dusting
¾ cup plus 2 tablespoons whole wheat bread flour
1 tablespoon skim milk powder

1½ teaspoons salt
2 teaspoons soft light brown sugar
2 tablespoons butter, diced
1½ teaspoons instant dry yeast

1 Pour the water into the bread pan. Sprinkle each type of flour over in turn, covering the water completely. Sprinkle the milk powder over the flour. Place the salt, sugar, and butter in separate corners of the pan. Make a small indent in the middle of the flour and add the yeast.

2 Close the lid and set the machine to "Basic White"/"Normal"(or equivalent), then select the loaf size and crust type. Press Start. If possible, 10 minutes before the baking cycle starts, brush the top of the loaf with water and dust with a little flour. Using a sharp knife, cut a slash, about ½ inch deep, along the length of the loaf.

3 After baking, remove the bread pan from the machine and turn the loaf out onto a wire rack to cool. Serve in slices.

honey-oatmeal bread

PREPARATION TIME 15 MINUTES, PLUS MIXING & KNEADING TIME IN BREAD MACHINE, PLUS RISING

COOKING TIME 30 TO 35 MINUTES   **MAKES** 1 LOAF (SERVES 12 TO 14)

1 cup water
7 tablespoons milk (at room temperature),
    plus extra for glazing
2 tablespoons honey
3½ cups whole wheat bread flour

heaped 1 cup rolled oats, plus extra
    for sprinkling
1½ teaspoons salt
1 teaspoon sugar
2 tablespoons butter, diced
1½ teaspoons instant dry yeast

1   Pour the water and milk into the bread pan, then add the honey. Sprinkle the flour over, covering the liquid completely. Sprinkle the oats over. Place the salt, sugar, and butter in separate corners of the pan. Make a small indent in the middle and add the yeast. Close the lid, set the machine to "Dough," and press Start.

2   Grease or flour a cookie sheet and set aside. When the dough is ready, remove it from the machine and punch it down on a lightly floured surface, then shape it into a ball. Place on the cookie sheet, cover, and leave to rise in a warm place until double in size.

3   Preheat the oven to 450°F. Slash the top of the loaf down the middle, brush with milk, and sprinkle with extra rolled oats.

4   Bake 10 minutes, then reduce the oven temperature to 400°F and bake 20 to 25 minutes longer, or until the bread is risen, light brown, and sounds hollow when tapped underneath. Transfer to a wire rack to cool. Serve in slices.

malted whole grain cobb

PREPARATION TIME 15 MINUTES, PLUS MIXING & KNEADING TIME IN BREAD MACHINE, PLUS RISING
COOKING TIME 30 TO 35 MINUTES   **MAKES** 1 LARGE LOAF (SERVES 14 TO 16)

1 cup water
7 tablespoons milk (at room temperature),
    plus extra for glazing
2 tablespoons malt extract
1¾ cups mixed-grain flour
1¾ cups plus 2½ tablespoons whole wheat
    bread flour

1½ teaspoons salt
2 teaspoons sugar
2 tablespoons butter, diced
1½ teaspoons instant dry yeast
kibbled or cracked wheat for sprinkling

1   Pour the water and milk into the bread pan, then add the malt extract. Sprinkle each type of flour over
    in turn, covering the liquid completely. Place the salt, sugar, and butter in separate corners of the pan.
    Make a small indent in the middle of the flour and add the yeast. Close the lid, set the machine to
    "Dough," and press Start.
2   Grease or flour a cookie sheet and set aside. When the dough is ready, remove it from the machine
    and punch it down on a lightly floured surface, then shape it into a large ball. Place on the cookie
    sheet, cover, and leave to rise in a warm place until double in size.
3   Preheat the oven to 450°F. Cut a cross shape into the top of the loaf, brush with a little milk, and
    sprinkle with kibbled or cracked wheat.
4   Bake 10 minutes, then reduce the oven temperature to 400°F and bake 20 to 25 minutes longer, or
    until the bread is risen, light brown, and sounds hollow when tapped underneath. Transfer to a wire
    rack to cool. Serve in slices.

french bread

PREPARATION TIME 15 MINUTES, PLUS MIXING & KNEADING TIME IN BREAD MACHINE, PLUS RISING
COOKING TIME 15 TO 20 MINUTES   **MAKES** 2 FRENCH STICKS (EACH LOAF SERVES 4 TO 6)

1¼ cups water
2¾ cups plus 2 tablespoons white bread flour
⅓ cup plus 1 tablespoon all-purpose flour

1½ teaspoons salt
1 teaspoon sugar
1 teaspoon instant dry yeast

1   Pour the water into the bread pan. Sprinkle each type of flour over in turn, covering the water completely. Place the salt and sugar in separate corners of the pan. Make a small indent in the middle of the flour and add the yeast. Close the lid, set the machine to "French Dough" (or equivalent), and press Start.

2   Meanwhile, flour a large cookie sheet and set aside. When the dough is ready, remove it from the machine and punch it down on a lightly floured surface, then divide it in half and roll out each portion to make a rectangle about 8 x 3 inches in size. Starting from a long edge, carefully roll up each rectangle of dough like a jelly roll.

3   Gently roll and stretch each piece of dough to make a loaf 11 to 13 inches long. Place the loaves between the folds of a pleated dish towel for support, cover, and leave to rise in a warm place until double in size.

4   Preheat the oven to 425°F. Roll the loaves onto the cookie sheet. Using a sharp knife, cut several diagonal slashes in the top of each loaf at regular intervals. Spray the inside of the hot oven with water, then immediately bake the loaves 15 to 20 minutes, or until crisp and golden brown. Transfer to a wire rack to cool. Serve warm or cold.

caraway-cheese loaf

PREPARATION TIME 15 MINUTES, PLUS MIXING & KNEADING TIME IN BREAD MACHINE, PLUS RISING
COOKING TIME 30 MINUTES   **MAKES** 1 LOAF (SERVES 10 TO 12)

1¼ cups milk (at room temperature), plus extra
for glazing
3¼ cups white bread flour
2 teaspoons mustard powder
1 tablespoon caraway seeds

2 tablespoons freshly grated Parmesan cheese
1 cup finely grated sharp Cheddar cheese
1¼ teaspoons salt
1½ teaspoons sugar
1½ teaspoons instant dry yeast

1   Pour the milk into the bread pan. Sprinkle the flour over, covering the milk completely, then sprinkle
the mustard powder, 2 teaspoons of the caraway seeds, the Parmesan cheese, and ⅔ cup of the
Cheddar cheese over. Place the salt and sugar in separate corners of the pan. Make a small indent in
the middle of the flour and add the yeast. Close the lid, set the machine to "Dough," and press Start.

2   Meanwhile, grease or flour a cookie sheet and set aside. When the dough is ready, remove it from
the machine and punch it down on a lightly floured surface, then shape the dough into a 6-inch ball
and place on the cookie sheet. Cover and leave to rise in a warm place until double in size.

3   Preheat the oven to 450°F. Using a sharp knife, cut a shallow cross in the top of the loaf, then brush
with a little milk. Mix together the remaining caraway seeds and Cheddar cheese and sprinkle over
the top of the loaf.

4   Bake the loaf 10 minutes, then reduce the oven temperature to 400°F and bake 20 minutes longer,
or until the bread is risen, golden brown, and sounds hollow when tapped underneath. Cover the loaf
loosely with foil halfway through the cooking time if it is browning too much. Transfer to a wire rack
to cool. Serve in slices.

caraway seed bread

PREPARATION TIME 10 MINUTES   **COOKING TIME** VARIES ACCORDING TO BREAD MACHINE

MAKES 1 LOAF (SERVES 10)

1½ cups water

2 tablespoons honey

3 cups whole wheat bread flour

¾ cup plus 1½ tablespoons white bread flour

2 tablespoons caraway seeds

2 tablespoons skim milk powder

1½ teaspoons salt

2 tablespoons butter, diced

1 teaspoon instant dry yeast

1   Pour the water into the bread pan, then add the honey. Sprinkle each type of flour over in turn, covering the liquid completely. Sprinkle the caraway seeds over the flour, then sprinkle the milk powder over the seeds. Place the salt and butter in separate corners of the pan. Make a small indent in the middle of the flour and add the yeast.

2   Close the lid and set the machine to "Multigrain" or "Whole Wheat" (or equivalent), then select the loaf size and crust type. Press Start.

3   After baking, remove the bread pan from the machine and turn the loaf out onto a wire rack to cool. Serve in slices.

Variations Use cumin or fennel seeds in place of caraway seeds. Use maple syrup in place of honey.

seeded rye bread

PREPARATION TIME 10 MINUTES   **COOKING TIME** VARIES ACCORDING TO BREAD MACHINE

MAKES 1 LOAF (SERVES 10)

1½ cups water
1 tablespoon honey
2¾ cups plus 2 tablespoons white bread flour
¾ cup rye flour
2 tablespoons caraway seeds

2 tablespoons skim milk powder
1½ teaspoons salt
2 tablespoons butter, diced
1 teaspoon instant dry yeast

1 Pour the water into the bread pan, then add the honey. Sprinkle each type of flour over in turn, covering the liquid completely. Sprinkle the caraway seeds over the flour, then sprinkle the milk powder over the seeds. Place the salt and butter in separate corners of the pan. Make a small indent in the middle of the flour and add the yeast.

2 Close the lid and set the machine to "Basic White"/"Normal" (or equivalent), then select the loaf size and crust type. Press Start.

3 After baking, remove the bread pan from the machine and turn the loaf out onto a wire rack to cool. Serve in slices.

sunflower seed loaf (pictured right)

PREPARATION TIME 10 MINUTES   **COOKING TIME** VARIES ACCORDING TO BREAD MACHINE

MAKES 1 LOAF (SERVES 10)

1¼ cups water
2 tablespoons sunflower oil
1⅔ cups white bread flour
1⅔ cups mixed-grain flour
1 tablespoon skim milk powder

1½ teaspoons salt
2 teaspoons sugar
1 teaspoon instant dry yeast
5 tablespoons sunflower seeds

1 Pour the water into the bread pan, then add the oil. Sprinkle each type of flour over in turn, covering the liquid completely. Sprinkle the milk powder over the flour. Place the salt and sugar in separate corners of the pan. Make a small indent in the middle of the flour and add the yeast.

2 Close the lid and set the machine to "Basic White"/"Normal," with "Raisin," if available (or equivalent), then select the loaf size and crust type. Press Start.

3 Add the sunflower seeds when the machine makes a sound (beeps) to add extra ingredients during the kneading cycle. (Or add 5 minutes before the end of the kneading cycle.)

4 After baking, remove the bread pan from the machine and turn the loaf out onto a wire rack to cool. Serve in slices.

six-seed bread

PREPARATION TIME 10 MINUTES   **COOKING TIME** VARIES ACCORDING TO BREAD MACHINE

MAKES 1 LOAF (SERVES 10)

1¼ cups water

2 tablespoons sunflower oil

1⅔ cups white bread flour

heaped 1¾ cups whole wheat bread flour

1 tablespoon skim milk powder

1½ teaspoons salt

2 teaspoons sugar

1 teaspoon instant dry yeast

2 tablespoons sunflower seeds

1 tablespoon pumpkin seeds

2 teaspoons sesame seeds

2 teaspoons poppy seeds

1 teaspoon caraway seeds

1 teaspoon cumin or fennel seeds

1   Pour the water into the bread pan, then add the oil. Sprinkle each type of flour over in turn, covering the liquid completely. Sprinkle the milk powder over the flour. Place the salt and sugar in separate corners of the pan. Make a small indent in the middle of the flour and add the yeast.

2   Close the lid and set the machine to "Basic White"/"Normal," with "Raisin," if available (or equivalent), then select the loaf size and crust type. Press Start.

3   Combine the seeds. Add the mixed seeds when the machine makes a sound (beeps) to add extra ingredients during the kneading cycle. (Or add 5 minutes before the end of the kneading cycle.)

4   After baking, remove the bread pan from the machine and turn the loaf out onto a wire rack to cool. Serve in slices.

Variation Packages of prepared mixed seeds suitable for breadmaking are available. Use 5 tablespoons mixed seeds in place of the seeds listed above.

cheese & sesame seed cobb

PREPARATION TIME 15 MINUTES, PLUS MIXING & KNEADING TIME IN BREAD MACHINE, PLUS RISING

COOKING TIME 35 TO 45 MINUTES   **MAKES** 1 LOAF (SERVES 10)

1¼ cups milk (at room temperature), plus extra
    for glazing
3¼ cups white bread flour
2 teaspoons mustard powder
a few turns of freshly ground black pepper
⅔ cup finely grated Gruyère or Swiss cheese

1¼ teaspoons salt
1½ teaspoons sugar
2 tablespoons butter, diced
1½ teaspoons instant dry yeast
sesame seeds for sprinkling

1   Pour the milk into the bread pan. Sprinkle the flour over, covering the milk completely, then sprinkle
the mustard powder, black pepper, and cheese over. Place the salt, sugar, and butter in separate
corners of the pan. Make a small indent in the middle of the flour and add the yeast. Close the lid,
set the machine to "Dough," and press Start.

2   Meanwhile, grease or flour a cookie sheet and set aside. When the dough is ready, remove it from
the machine and punch it down on a lightly floured surface, then shape the dough into a flat ball and
place on the cookie sheet. Cover and leave to rise in a warm place until double in size.

3   Preheat the oven to 375°F. Lightly brush the top of the loaf with milk and sprinkle with sesame seeds.

4   Bake 35 to 45 minutes, or until the bread is risen, golden brown, and sounds hollow when tapped
underneath. Transfer to a wire rack to cool. Serve in slices.

garden herb bread

PREPARATION TIME 10 MINUTES   **COOKING TIME** VARIES ACCORDING TO BREAD MACHINE

MAKES 1 LOAF (SERVES 10)

1½ cups water
3½ cups white bread flour
1 tablespoon skim milk powder
2 tablespoons chopped fresh parsley
2 tablespoons snipped fresh chives

2 teaspoons chopped fresh thyme
1½ teaspoons salt
2 teaspoons sugar
2 tablespoons butter, diced
1 teaspoon instant dry yeast

1   Pour the water into the bread pan. Sprinkle the flour over, covering the water completely. Sprinkle the milk powder over the flour. Combine the herbs, then sprinkle them over the milk powder. Place the salt, sugar, and butter in separate corners of the pan. Make a small indent in the middle of the flour and add the yeast.

2   Close the lid and set the machine to "Basic White"/"Normal" (or equivalent), then select the loaf size and crust type. Press Start.

3   After baking, remove the bread pan from the machine and turn the loaf out onto a wire rack to cool. Serve in slices.

Variation Use 2 tablespoons chopped cilantro or fresh basil in place of the thyme.

malted wheat bread (pictured right)

PREPARATION TIME 10 MINUTES   **COOKING TIME** VARIES ACCORDING TO BREAD MACHINE
MAKES 1 LOAF (SERVES 10)

1¼ cups water
2 tablespoons malt extract
3¼ cups mixed-grain flour
1 tablespoon skim milk powder

1½ teaspoons salt
2 teaspoons sugar
2 tablespoons butter, diced
1 teaspoon instant dry yeast

1   Pour the water into the bread pan, then add the malt extract. Sprinkle the flour over, covering the liquid completely. Sprinkle the milk powder over the flour. Place the salt, sugar, and butter in separate corners of the pan. Make a small indent in the middle of the flour and add the yeast.

2   Close the lid and set the machine to "Whole Wheat" or "Multigrain" (or equivalent), then select the loaf size and crust type. Press Start.

3   After baking, remove the bread pan from the machine and turn the loaf out onto a wire rack to cool. Serve in slices.

whole wheat herb loaf

PREPARATION TIME 10 MINUTES   **COOKING TIME** VARIES ACCORDING TO BREAD MACHINE
MAKES 1 LOAF (SERVES 8 TO 10)

1¼ cups water
3½ cups whole wheat bread flour
1 tablespoon skim milk powder
1 tablespoon chopped fresh mixed herbs,
      such as chives, sage, and marjoram
1 tablespoon chopped fresh parsley

1½ teaspoons freshly ground black pepper
2 teaspoons salt
2 teaspoons sugar
2 tablespoons butter, diced
1½ teaspoons instant dry yeast

1   Pour the water into the bread pan. Sprinkle the flour over, covering the water completely. Sprinkle the milk powder over the flour. Combine the herbs and black pepper, then sprinkle these over the milk powder. Place the salt, sugar, and butter in separate corners of the pan. Make a small indent in the middle of the flour and add the yeast.

2   Close the lid and set the machine to "Whole Wheat" (or equivalent), then select the loaf size and crust type. Press Start.

3   After baking, remove the bread pan from the machine and turn the loaf out onto a wire rack to cool. Serve in slices.

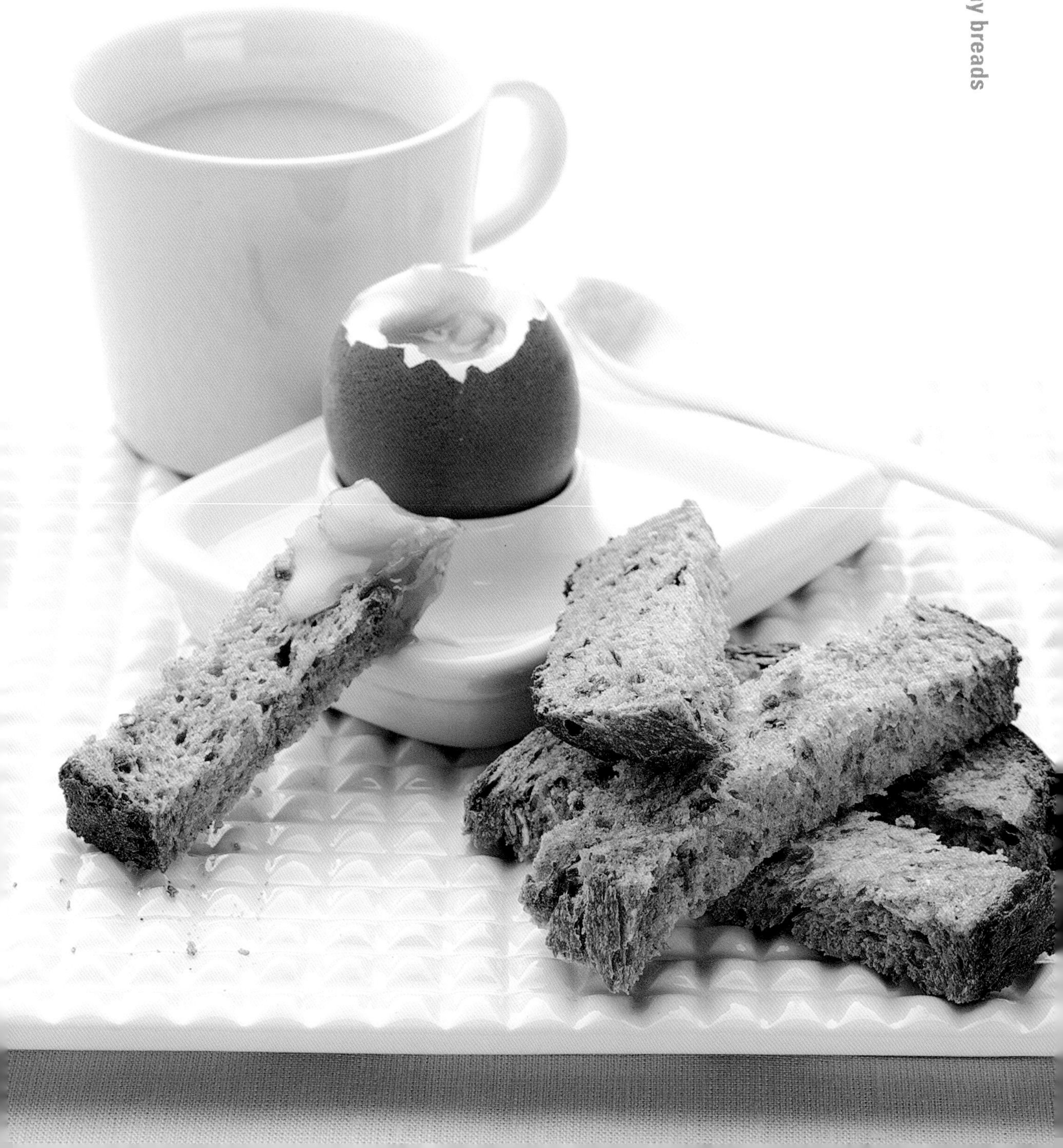

flowerpot breads

PREPARATION TIME 15 MINUTES, PLUS MIXING & KNEADING TIME IN BREAD MACHINE, PLUS RISING
COOKING TIME 30 TO 40 MINUTES   **MAKES** 2 LOAVES (EACH LOAF SERVES 4)

vegetable oil for greasing
1¼ cups water
1 tablespoon malt extract
3½ cups whole wheat bread flour
1⅓ cups barley flakes, plus extra for sprinkling
1 to 2 tablespoons chopped fresh mixed herbs

1½ teaspoons salt
2 teaspoons sugar
2 tablespoons butter, diced
2 teaspoons instant dry yeast
milk for glazing

1   Liberally brush 2 new terracotta flowerpots (about 5½ inches in diameter and 4½ inches high)
    with vegetable oil, inside and out, then bake in a hot oven (400°F) about 30 minutes. Leave the pots
    to cool, then repeat this process until they are impregnated with oil. Do not wash after use: wipe
    clean with paper towels. Lightly grease the pots and set aside.

2   Pour the water into the bread pan and add the malt extract. Sprinkle the flour over, covering the
    liquid completely, then sprinkle the barley flakes and herbs over. Place the salt, sugar, and butter in
    separate corners of the pan. Make a small indent in the middle of the flour and add the yeast. Close
    the lid, set the machine to "Dough," and press Start.

3   When the dough is ready, remove it from the machine, punch it down on a lightly floured surface
    and divide it in half. Shape and fit each piece of dough into a flowerpot—the dough should roughly
    half-fill the pots.

4   Cover and leave to rise in a warm place 45 to 60 minutes, or until the dough almost reaches the top of
    the flowerpots.

5   Preheat the oven to 400°F. Brush the loaf tops with a little milk and sprinkle with extra barley flakes.
    Bake 30 to 40 minutes, or until the bread is risen and sounds hollow when turned out and tapped
    underneath. Place on a wire rack to cool. Serve in slices.

herb flutes

PREPARATION TIME 15 MINUTES, PLUS MIXING & KNEADING TIME IN BREAD MACHINE, PLUS RISING
COOKING TIME 25 MINUTES   **MAKES** 2 LOAVES (EACH LOAF SERVES 4 TO 6)

1 cup plus 2 tablespoons water
2 tablespoons olive oil
3¼ cups white bread flour, plus extra for dusting
1 tablespoon dried herbes de Provence

⅓ cup freshly grated Parmesan cheese
1¼ teaspoons salt
1½ teaspoons sugar
1½ teaspoons instant dry yeast

1   Pour the water into the bread pan, then add the oil. Sprinkle the flour over, covering the liquid completely, then sprinkle the dried herbs and cheese over. Place the salt and sugar in separate corners of the pan. Make a small indent in the middle of the flour and add the yeast. Close the lid, set the machine to "Dough," and press Start.

2   Meanwhile, grease or flour a large cookie sheet and set aside. When the dough is ready, remove it from the machine and punch it down on a lightly floured surface, then divide it in half and shape each half into a baton about 12 inches long. Place on the cookie sheet, cover, and leave to rise in a warm place about 45 minutes, or until double in size.

3   Preheat the oven to 425°F. Dust each loaf with a little flour, then, using a sharp knife, slash across the top of each loaf 4 times diagonally at regular intervals.

4   Bake about 25 minutes, or until the bread is risen, golden brown, and sounds hollow when tapped underneath. Transfer to a wire rack to cool. Serve warm or cold.

milk loaf

PREPARATION TIME 10 MINUTES   **COOKING TIME** VARIES ACCORDING TO BREAD MACHINE

MAKES 1 LOAF (SERVES 10)

7 ounces milk (at room temperature)

7 tablespoons water

3⅓ cups white bread flour

1½ teaspoons salt

2 teaspoons sugar

2 tablespoons butter, diced

1 teaspoon instant dry yeast

1   Pour the milk and water into the bread pan. Sprinkle the flour over, covering the liquid completely. Place the salt, sugar, and butter in separate corners of the pan. Make a small indent in the middle of the flour and add the yeast.

2   Close the lid and set the machine to "Basic White"/"Normal" (or equivalent), then select the loaf size and crust type. Press Start.

3   After baking, remove the bread pan from the machine and turn the loaf out onto a wire rack to cool. Serve in slices.

barley bread

PREPARATION TIME 15 MINUTES, PLUS MIXING & KNEADING TIME IN BREAD MACHINE, PLUS RISING
COOKING TIME 30 TO 35 MINUTES   **MAKES** 1 LOAF (SERVES 10 TO 12)

1½ cups water
3 cups whole wheat bread flour
1 cup barley flour

2 teaspoons salt
2 teaspoons sugar
1½ teaspoons instant dry yeast

1   Pour the water into the bread pan. Sprinkle each type of flour over in turn, covering the water completely. Place the salt and sugar in separate corners of the pan. Make a small indent in the middle of the flour and add the yeast. Close the lid, set the machine to "Dough," and press Start.

2   Meanwhile, grease a 9- x 5-inch loaf pan and set aside. When the dough is ready, remove it from the machine and punch it down on a lightly floured surface, then shape the dough into an oblong. Place in the loaf pan, cover, and leave to rise in a warm place until double in size.

3   Preheat the oven to 450°F. Bake 10 minutes, then reduce the oven temperature to 400°F and bake 20 to 25 minutes longer, or until the bread is risen, light brown, and sounds hollow when turned out and tapped underneath. Cool on a wire rack. Serve in slices.

sun-dried tomato bread (pictured left)

PREPARATION TIME 10 MINUTES   **COOKING TIME** VARIES ACCORDING TO BREAD MACHINE
MAKES 1 LOAF (SERVES 8 TO 10)

1¼ cups water
1 tablespoon oil from a jar of sun-dried tomatoes
3⅓ cups white bread flour
⅓ cup freshly grated Parmesan cheese
1½ teaspoons salt

2 teaspoons sugar
1 teaspoon instant dry yeast
½ cup sun-dried tomatoes in oil, patted dry
    and chopped

1   Pour the water into the bread pan, then add the oil. Sprinkle the flour over, covering the liquid completely. Sprinkle the Parmesan cheese over. Place the salt and sugar in separate corners of the pan. Make a small indent in the middle of the flour and add the yeast.

2   Close the lid and set the machine to "Basic White"/"Normal," with "Raisin," if available (or equivalent), then select the loaf size and crust type. Press Start.

3   Add the sun-dried tomatoes when the machine makes a sound (beeps) to add extra ingredients during the kneading cycle. (Or add 5 minutes before the end of the kneading cycle.)

4   After baking, remove the bread pan from the machine and turn the loaf out onto a wire rack to cool. Serve in slices.

pesto whirl bread

PREPARATION TIME 20 MINUTES, PLUS MIXING & KNEADING TIME IN BREAD MACHINE, PLUS RISING
COOKING TIME 25 TO 30 MINUTES   **MAKES** 1 LOAF (SERVES 10 TO 12)

1¼ cups plus 2 tablespoons water
2 tablespoons olive oil
3½ cups white bread flour
1 teaspoon salt

1 teaspoon sugar
1 teaspoon instant dry yeast
4 tablespoons store-bought green pesto sauce

1   Pour the water into the bread pan, then add the oil. Sprinkle the flour over, covering the liquid
    completely. Place the salt and sugar in separate corners of the pan. Make a small indent in the middle
    of the flour and add the yeast. Close the lid, set the machine to "Dough," and press Start.
2   Meanwhile, grease a 9- x 5-inch loaf pan and set aside. When the dough is ready, remove it from the
    machine and punch it down on a lightly floured surface, then roll or pat out to form a rectangle about
    12 x 8 inches in size.
3   Spread the pesto evenly over the rectangle of dough, then roll up the dough fairly tightly, like a
    jelly roll, starting from a short side. Reshape slightly, if necessary, and place in the loaf pan.
    Cover and leave to rise in a warm place 30 to 45 minutes, or until double in size.
4   Preheat the oven to 425°F. Bake 25 to 30 minutes, or until the loaf is risen and golden. Turn out and
    cool on a wire rack. Serve in slices on its own or spread with butter.

Variation Use red pesto sauce in place of traditional green pesto sauce.

greek black olive bread

PREPARATION TIME 20 MINUTES, PLUS MIXING & KNEADING TIME IN BREAD MACHINE, PLUS RISING
COOKING TIME 30 TO 35 MINUTES   **MAKES** 1 LOAF (SERVES 10 TO 12)

1¼ cups plus 2 tablespoons water
2 tablespoons extra-virgin olive oil
3½ cups white bread flour, plus extra for dusting
1 teaspoon salt

1 teaspoon sugar
1 teaspoon instant dry yeast
¾ cup pitted black olives, chopped

1 Pour the water into the bread pan, then add the oil. Sprinkle the flour over, covering the liquid completely. Place the salt and sugar in separate corners of the pan. Make a small indent in the middle of the flour and add the yeast. Close the lid, set the machine to "Dough," and press Start.

2 Meanwhile, grease or flour a cookie sheet and set aside. When the dough is ready, remove it from the machine and punch it down on a well-floured surface, then knead in about half of the chopped olives. Roll out to form a rectangle about 14 x 10 inches in size.

3 Sprinkle the surface of the dough evenly with the remaining olives, then roll up the dough fairly tightly, like a jelly roll, starting from a short side. Pinch the edges of each end together to seal. Place the loaf, seam-side down, on the cookie sheet. Cover and leave to rise in a warm place until double in size.

4 Preheat the oven to 425°F. Dust the loaf with a little sifted flour. Bake 10 minutes, then reduce the oven temperature to 375°F and bake 20 to 25 minutes longer, or until the bread is risen, golden brown, and sounds hollow when tapped underneath. Transfer to a wire rack to cool. Serve warm or cold in slices.

braided herb bread

PREPARATION TIME 20 MINUTES, PLUS MIXING & KNEADING TIME IN BREAD MACHINE, PLUS RISING
COOKING TIME 35 TO 45 MINUTES **MAKES** 1 LOAF (SERVES 10)

⅔ cup water
⅔ cup milk (at room temperature),
    plus extra for glazing
3¼ cups white bread flour
1 tablespoon dried herbes de Provence

⅔ cup finely grated sharp Cheddar or
    Monterey Jack cheese
1¼ teaspoons salt
1½ teaspoons sugar
2 tablespoons butter, diced
1½ teaspoons instant dry yeast

1 Pour the water and milk into the bread pan. Sprinkle the flour over, covering the liquid completely, then sprinkle the dried herbs and cheese over. Place the salt, sugar, and butter in separate corners of the pan. Make a small indent in the middle of the flour and add the yeast. Close the lid, set the machine to "Dough," and press Start.

2 Meanwhile, grease or flour a cookie sheet and set aside. When the dough is ready, remove it from the machine and punch it down on a lightly floured surface, then divide it in half. Roll each piece of dough into a rope shape. Place them side by side and pinch together at one end to seal.

3 Loosely braid the ropes of dough together, then pinch them together at the other end. Place the braid on the cookie sheet. Cover and leave to rise in a warm place until double in size.

4 Preheat the oven to 375°F. Lightly brush the braid with milk. Bake 35 to 45 minutes, or until the bread is risen, golden brown, and sounds hollow when tapped underneath. Transfer to a wire rack to cool. Serve in slices.

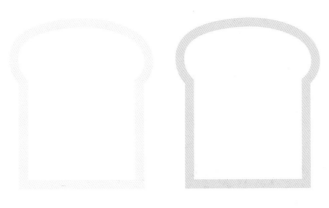

cheese & poppy seed braid

PREPARATION TIME 15 MINUTES, PLUS MIXING & KNEADING TIME IN BREAD MACHINE, PLUS RISING

COOKING TIME 30 TO 40 MINUTES   **MAKES** 1 LOAF (SERVES 10)

1¼ cups milk (at room temperature), plus extra
    for glazing
3¼ cups white bread flour
2 teaspoons mustard powder
a few turns of freshly ground black pepper
⅔ cup finely grated sharp Cheddar cheese

1¼ teaspoons salt
1½ teaspoons sugar
2 tablespoons butter, diced
1½ teaspoons instant dry yeast
poppy seeds for sprinkling

1   Pour the milk into the bread pan. Sprinkle the flour over, covering the milk completely, then sprinkle
    the mustard powder, black pepper, and cheese over. Place the salt, sugar, and butter in separate
    corners of the pan. Make a small indent in the middle of the flour and add the yeast. Close the lid,
    set the machine to "Dough," and press Start.

2   Meanwhile, grease or flour a cookie sheet and set aside. When the dough is ready, remove it from
    the machine and punch it down on a lightly floured surface, then divide it in half. Roll each piece of
    dough into a rope shape. Pinch them together at one end to seal.

3   Loosely braid the ropes of dough together, then pinch them together at the other end. Place the braid
    on the cookie sheet. Cover and leave to rise in a warm place until double in size.

4   Preheat the oven to 375°F. Brush the braid with a little milk and sprinkle with poppy seeds.

5   Bake 30 to 40 minutes, or until the bread is risen, golden brown, and sounds hollow when tapped
    underneath. Transfer to a wire rack to cool. Serve in slices.

cheese & grain cobb

PREPARATION TIME 15 MINUTES, PLUS MIXING & KNEADING TIME IN BREAD MACHINE, PLUS RISING

COOKING TIME 35 TO 45 MINUTES   **MAKES** 1 LOAF (SERVES 10 TO 12)

1¼ cups milk (at room temperature), plus extra
  for glazing
heaped 1¾ cups whole wheat bread flour
1⅔ cups mixed-grain flour
2 teaspoons mustard powder
a few turns of freshly ground black pepper

⅔ cup finely grated sharp Cheddar cheese
1½ teaspoons salt
1½ teaspoons sugar
2 tablespoons butter, diced
1½ teaspoons instant dry yeast
kibbled or cracked wheat for sprinkling

1   Pour the milk into the bread pan. Sprinkle the flour over, covering the milk completely, then sprinkle the mustard powder, black pepper, and cheese over. Place the salt, sugar, and butter in separate corners of the pan. Make a small indent in the middle of the flour and add the yeast. Close the lid, set the machine to "Dough," and press Start.

2   Meanwhile, grease or flour a cookie sheet and set aside. When the dough is ready, remove it from the machine and punch it down on a lightly floured surface, then shape the dough into a flat ball and place on the cookie sheet. Cover and leave to rise in a warm place 30 to 45 minutes, or until double in size.

3   Preheat the oven to 375°F. Lightly brush the top of the loaf with milk, then sprinkle with kibbled or cracked wheat.

4   Bake 35 to 45 minutes, or until the bread is risen, golden brown, and sounds hollow when tapped underneath. Transfer to a wire rack to cool. Serve in slices.

garlic bubble ring

PREPARATION TIME 20 MINUTES, PLUS MIXING & KNEADING TIME IN BREAD MACHINE, PLUS RISING
COOKING TIME 30 TO 40 MINUTES   **MAKES** 1 LOAF (SERVES 12)

1¼ cups plus 2 tablespoons warm water
   (or according to bread-mix package directions)
1 package (1 lb. 2 oz.) white bread mix
7 tablespoons butter, melted
1 egg, beaten

2 tablespoons freshly grated Parmesan cheese
2 cloves garlic, crushed
½ teaspoon salt
1 teaspoon dried mixed herbs

1 Pour the correct amount of water into the bread pan. Sprinkle the bread mix over, covering the water completely. Close the lid, set the machine to "Dough," and press Start. Meanwhile, grease a 9-inch loose-bottomed springform pan fitted with a tube bottom, or a ring mold, and set aside.

2 When the dough is ready, remove it from the machine and punch it down on a lightly floured surface, then divide it into 12 equal portions and roll each piece into a ball.

3 Combine the melted butter, egg, cheese, garlic, salt, and dried herbs in a small bowl, mixing well. Dip the dough balls into the mixture, coating them liberally all over, then arrange them in a single layer in the pan. Drizzle any remaining butter mixture over. Cover and leave to rise in a warm place until double in size.

4 Preheat the oven to 375°F. Bake 30 to 40 minutes, or until the bread is risen and golden brown. Turn out and cool on a wire rack. Pull the rolls apart to serve warm or cold.

cheese & olive bread

PREPARATION TIME 10 MINUTES   **COOKING TIME** VARIES ACCORDING TO BREAD MACHINE

MAKES 1 LOAF (SERVES 8 TO 10)

1¼ cups water
1 tablespoon extra-virgin olive oil
3¼ cups white bread flour
½ cup freshly grated Parmesan cheese
2 teaspoons dried mixed herbs

1½ teaspoons salt
2 teaspoons sugar
1 teaspoon instant dry yeast
⅓ cup mixed pitted black and green
    olives, chopped

1 Pour the water into the bread pan, then add the oil. Sprinkle the flour over, covering the liquid
   completely. Sprinkle the Parmesan cheese and dried mixed herbs over. Place the salt and sugar
   in separate corners of the pan. Make a small indent in the middle of the flour and add the yeast.

2 Close the lid and set the machine to "Basic White"/"Normal," with "Raisin," if available (or
   equivalent), then select the loaf size and crust type. Press Start.

3 Add the mixed olives when the machine makes a sound (beeps) to add extra ingredients during
   the kneading cycle. (Or add 5 minutes before the end of the kneading cycle.)

4 After baking, remove the bread pan from the machine and turn the loaf out onto a wire rack to cool.
   Serve in slices.

golden cheesy breads

PREPARATION TIME 15 MINUTES, PLUS MIXING & KNEADING TIME IN BREAD MACHINE, PLUS RISING

COOKING TIME 20 TO 25 MINUTES   **MAKES** 4 SMALL LOAVES (EACH LOAF SERVES 1 TO 2)

1¼ cups milk (at room temperature), plus extra
    for glazing
3¼ cups white bread flour
1 teaspoon mustard powder
1⅔ cups grated Gouda cheese

1¼ teaspoons salt
1½ teaspoons sugar
2 tablespoons butter, diced
1½ teaspoons instant dry yeast

1   Pour the milk into the bread pan. Sprinkle the flour over, covering the milk completely, then sprinkle the mustard powder and two-thirds of the cheese over. Place the salt, sugar, and butter in separate corners of the pan. Make a small indent in the middle of the flour and add the yeast. Close the lid, set the machine to "Dough," and press Start.

2   Meanwhile, grease or flour 2 cookie sheets and set aside. When the dough is ready, remove it from the machine and punch it down on a lightly floured surface, then divide it into 4 equal portions. Shape each portion into a ball or oval and place on the cookie sheets. Cover and leave to rise in a warm place until double in size.

3   Preheat the oven to 400°F. Lightly brush the tops of the loaves with a little milk, then sprinkle the remaining cheese over.

4   Bake 20 to 25 minutes, or until the bread is risen, golden brown, and sounds hollow when tapped underneath. Cover the loaves loosely with foil toward the end of the cooking time if they are browning too much. Transfer to a wire rack to cool.

sesame ring breads

PREPARATION TIME 15 MINUTES, PLUS MIXING & KNEADING TIME IN BREAD MACHINE, PLUS RISING
COOKING TIME 10 TO 15 MINUTES   **MAKES** 8 RING BREADS

1 cup water
3 tablespoons unrefined or cold-pressed sesame oil
1 tablespoon honey
3¼ cups white bread flour
1½ teaspoons salt

2 teaspoons sugar
1 package (¼ oz.) instant dry yeast
beaten egg for glazing
sesame seeds for sprinkling

1   Pour the water into a bowl, add the oil and honey, and whisk well. Pour the mixture into the bread pan. Sprinkle the flour over, covering the liquid completely. Place the salt and sugar in separate corners of the pan. Make a small indent in the middle of the flour and add the yeast. Close the lid, set the machine to "Dough," and press Start.

2   Meanwhile, grease or flour 2 cookie sheets and set aside. When the dough is ready, remove it from the machine and punch it down on a lightly floured surface, then divide it into 8 equal portions.

3   Roll each portion into a rope shape about 12 inches long. Form each rope of dough into a ring and press the ends firmly together to seal. Place on the cookie sheets, spacing them well apart. Cover and leave to rise in a warm place until double in size.

4   Preheat the oven to 400°F. Lightly brush the dough rings with a little beaten egg and sprinkle with sesame seeds.

5   Bake 10 to 15 minutes, or until risen and golden brown. Transfer to a wire rack to cool. Serve warm.

herby polenta bread

PREPARATION TIME 10 MINUTES   **COOKING TIME** VARIES ACCORDING TO BREAD MACHINE
MAKES 1 LOAF (SERVES 10)

1¼ cups water
3 tablespoons honey
3 tablespoons chopped fresh mixed herbs,
    such as flat-leaf parsley, chives, and basil
⅓ cup polenta

2⅔ cups whole wheat bread flour
¾ cup plus 1½ tablespoons white bread flour
1½ teaspoons salt
2 tablespoons butter, diced
1½ teaspoons instant dry yeast

1 Pour the water into the bread pan, then add the honey. Sprinkle the chopped herbs and polenta over, then sprinkle each type of flour over in turn, covering the liquid completely. Place the salt and butter in separate corners of the pan. Make a small indent in the middle of the flour and add the yeast.

2 Close the lid and set the machine to "Whole Wheat" (or equivalent), then select the loaf size and crust type. Press Start.

3 After baking, remove the bread pan from the machine and turn the loaf out onto a wire rack to cool. Serve in slices.

Variation Use maple syrup in place of honey.

cheese & bacon bread

PREPARATION TIME 20 MINUTES   **COOKING TIME** VARIES ACCORDING TO BREAD MACHINE
MAKES 1 LOAF (SERVES 10)

1½ cups water
heaped 3¾ cups whole wheat bread flour
1½ tablespoons skim milk powder
1½ teaspoons salt
1 tablespoon sugar

1 teaspoon instant dry yeast
⅓ cup chopped cold, cooked, lean smoked
    back bacon
⅔ cup grated sharp Cheddar cheese

1   Pour the water into the bread pan. Sprinkle the flour over, covering the water completely.
    Sprinkle the milk powder over the flour. Place the salt and sugar in separate corners of the pan.
    Make a small indent in the middle of the flour and add the yeast.
2   Close the lid and set the machine to "Basic White"/"Normal," with "Raisin," if available (or
    equivalent), then select the loaf size and crust type. Press Start.
3   Combine the bacon and cheese. Add the bacon and cheese mixture when the machine makes a
    sound (beeps) to add extra ingredients during the kneading cycle. (Or add 5 minutes before the end
    of the kneading cycle.)
4   After baking, remove the bread pan from the machine and turn the loaf out onto a wire rack to cool.
    Serve in slices.

sausage & salsa "rolls"

PREPARATION TIME 20 MINUTES, PLUS MIXING & KNEADING TIME IN BREAD MACHINE, PLUS RISING

COOKING TIME 15 TO 20 MINUTES   **MAKES** 10 "ROLLS"

1¼ cups plus 2 tablespoons warm water
   (or according to bread-mix package directions)
1 package (1 lb. 2 oz.) white bread mix
½ cup finely grated sharp Cheddar cheese
a good pinch of cayenne pepper

10 cold, cooked, skinless thick link sausages of your
   choice (pork, beef, herby, spicy, and so on)
20 teaspoons tomato salsa (2 teaspoons per roll)
beaten egg for glazing

1   Pour the correct amount of water into the bread pan. Sprinkle the bread mix over, covering the water
    completely, then sprinkle the cheese and cayenne pepper over. Close the lid, set the machine to
    "Dough," and press Start.

2   Meanwhile, grease or flour 2 cookie sheets and set aside. When the dough is ready, remove it from
    the machine and punch it down on a lightly floured surface. Roll out the dough to form a 20- x 8-inch
    rectangle, then cut into ten 4-inch squares.

3   Place 1 sausage diagonally across 1 square of dough, then spread 2 teaspoons of salsa over the
    sausage. Fold the remaining 2 corners of the dough square over the sausage, pinching the edges
    together and pressing them down gently to seal: you will still be able to see both ends of the sausage.

4   Repeat with the remaining dough squares, sausages, and salsa, to make a total of 10 rolls. Place,
    seam-side up, on the cookie sheets, cover, and leave to rise in a warm place about 30 minutes, or
    until double in size.

5   Preheat the oven to 400°F. Lightly brush the rolls with a little beaten egg, then bake 15 to 20 minutes,
    or until risen and golden brown. Transfer to a wire rack to cool. Serve warm or cold.

CHAPTER 2

basic & everyday rolls

Bread rolls make for a quick-and-tasty treat any time of day; from warm, crusty rolls for breakfast to a wholesome, filling lunch, or an easy afternoon snack. In this chapter you will find a selection of delicious rolls, buns, knots, and bagels ideal for everyday eating.

Try Soft Whole Wheat Rolls, Floury White Buns, or Malted Country Rolls—perfect for lunchboxes. For breads with added flavors, choose from Rosemary Ciabatta Rolls and Golden Cheddar Knots, or seeded breads, such as Sesame Bagels and Poppy Seed Knots. And for a taste of the Mediterranean, try the Sun-Dried Tomato Rolls, Mediterranean Olive Bread Rolls, and Petits Pains au Lait.

breakfast rolls

PREPARATION TIME 15 MINUTES, PLUS MIXING & KNEADING TIME IN BREAD MACHINE, PLUS RISING
COOKING TIME 15 TO 20 MINUTES   **MAKES** 10 TO 12 ROLLS

⅔ cup milk (at room temperature), plus extra
 for glazing
⅔ cup water
3¼ cups white bread flour, plus extra for dusting

1½ teaspoons salt
2 teaspoons sugar
2 tablespoons butter, diced
1½ teaspoons instant dry yeast

1 Pour the milk and water into the bread pan. Sprinkle the flour over, covering the liquid completely.
Place the salt, sugar, and butter in separate corners of the pan. Make a small indent in the middle of
the flour and add the yeast. Close the lid, set the machine to "Dough," and press Start.

2 Meanwhile, grease or flour 2 cookie sheets and set aside. When the dough is ready, remove it from
the machine and punch it down on a lightly floured surface, then divide it into 10 to 12 equal portions.

3 Shape each portion of the dough into a ball or oval and place on the cookie sheets, spacing them well
apart. Cover and leave to rise in a warm place about 30 minutes, or until double in size.

4 Preheat the oven to 400°F. Lightly brush the rolls with milk and dust with flour. Bake 15 to 20 minutes,
or until light brown. Transfer to a wire rack to cool. Serve warm or cold.

dinner rolls

PREPARATION TIME 15 MINUTES, PLUS MIXING & KNEADING TIME IN BREAD MACHINE, PLUS RISING
COOKING TIME 15 TO 20 MINUTES   **MAKES** 12 ROLLS

1 cup milk (at room temperature)
1 egg, beaten
3 cups white bread flour
2 teaspoons salt
2 teaspoons sugar

4 tablespoons butter, diced
1 package (¼ oz.) instant dry yeast
poppy seeds or sesame seeds for sprinkling
 (optional)

1   Pour the milk into a bowl, add the egg, and whisk together. Pour the mixture into the bread pan.
    Sprinkle the flour over, covering the liquid completely. Add the salt, sugar, and butter in separate
    corners of the pan. Make a small indent in the middle of the flour and add the yeast. Close the lid, set
    the machine to "Dough," and press Start.

2   Meanwhile, grease or flour 2 cookie sheets and set aside. When the dough is ready, remove it from
    the machine and punch it down on a lightly floured surface, then divide it into 12 equal portions.

3   Form each portion of the dough into a ball, oval, or baton, or shape into a long rope and tie loosely in
    a single knot, pulling the ends through.

4   Place the rolls on the cookie sheets, spacing them well apart. Cover and leave to rise in a warm place
    about 30 minutes, or until double in size.

5   Preheat the oven to 425°F. Lightly brush the tops of the rolls with a little water and sprinkle with
    poppy or sesame seeds, if desired. Bake 15 to 20 minutes, or until risen and golden brown. Transfer
    to a wire rack to cool. Serve warm or cold.

soft whole wheat rolls

PREPARATION TIME 15 MINUTES, PLUS MIXING & KNEADING TIME IN BREAD MACHINE, PLUS RISING
COOKING TIME 10 TO 15 MINUTES **MAKES** 10 TO 12 ROLLS

⅔ cup water
⅔ cup milk (at room temperature)
2⅔ cups whole wheat bread flour, plus extra
    for dusting
¾ cup plus 1½ tablespoons white bread flour

1½ teaspoons salt
2 teaspoons sugar
2 tablespoons butter, diced
1½ teaspoons instant dry yeast

1   Pour the water and milk into the bread pan. Sprinkle each type of flour over in turn, covering the liquid completely. Add the salt, sugar, and butter in separate corners of the pan. Make a small indent in the middle of the flour and add the yeast. Close the lid, set the machine to "Dough," and press Start.

2   Meanwhile, grease or flour 2 cookie sheets and set aside. When the dough is ready, remove it from the machine and punch it down on a lightly floured surface, then divide it into 10 to 12 equal portions.

3   Shape each portion of the dough into a ball or oval, then press each one down firmly with the heel of your hand and release. Place the rolls on the cookie sheets, spacing them well apart, then cover and leave to rise in a warm place about 30 minutes, or until double in size.

4   Preheat the oven to 425°F. Lightly dust the tops of the rolls with wholewheat flour. Bake 10 to 15 minutes, or until light brown. Transfer to a wire rack to cool. Serve warm or cold.

floury white buns

PREPARATION TIME 15 MINUTES, PLUS MIXING & KNEADING TIME IN BREAD MACHINE, PLUS RISING
COOKING TIME 15 MINUTES   **MAKES** 10 BUNS

7 ounces milk (at room temperature), plus extra
    for glazing
½ cup water
3¼ cups white bread flour, plus extra for dusting

1½ teaspoons salt
2 teaspoons sugar
1 teaspoon instant dry yeast

1   Pour the milk and water into the bread pan. Sprinkle the flour over, covering the liquid completely.
Place the salt and sugar in separate corners of the pan. Make a small indent in the middle of the flour
and add the yeast. Close the lid, set the machine to "Dough," and press Start.

2   Meanwhile, grease or flour 2 cookie sheets and set aside. When the dough is ready, remove it from
the machine and punch it down on a lightly floured surface, then divide it into 10 equal portions.

3   Shape each portion of the dough into a flat ball, each about 3½ inches in diameter, and place on the
cookie sheets, spacing them well apart. Cover and leave to rise in a warm place about 30 minutes,
or until double in size.

4   Preheat the oven to 400°F. Gently press the middle of each bun to release any large air bubbles.
Lightly brush the buns with milk and dust with flour.

5   Bake about 15 minutes, or until light brown. Dust with a little more flour, then transfer to a wire rack
to cool. Serve warm or cold.

scottish buns

PREPARATION TIME 15 MINUTES, PLUS MIXING & KNEADING TIME IN BREAD MACHINE, PLUS RISING
COOKING TIME 15 TO 20 MINUTES   **MAKES** 10 BUNS

⅔ cup milk (at room temperature), plus extra
    for glazing
⅔ cup water
3¼ cups white bread flour, plus extra for dusting

1½ teaspoons salt
2 teaspoons sugar
1½ teaspoons instant dry yeast

1 Pour the milk and water into the bread pan. Sprinkle the flour over, covering the liquid completely.
   Place the salt and sugar in separate corners of the pan. Make a small indent in the middle of the flour
   and add the yeast. Close the lid, set the machine to "Dough," and press Start.

2 Meanwhile, grease or flour 2 cookie sheets and set aside. When the dough is ready, remove it from
   the machine and punch it down on a lightly floured surface, then divide it into 10 equal portions.

3 Roll or pat each portion of the dough into a flat ball or oval about ½ inch thick. Place on the cookie
   sheets, spacing them well apart, then cover and leave to rise in a warm place about 30 minutes,
   or until double in size.

4 Preheat the oven to 400°F. Gently press the middle of each bun to release any large air bubbles.
   Lightly brush the buns with milk and dust with flour.

5 Bake 15 to 20 minutes, or until light brown. Dust the tops with a little more flour, then transfer to a
   wire rack to cool. Serve warm.

rosemary ciabatta rolls

PREPARATION TIME 20 MINUTES, PLUS MIXING & KNEADING TIME IN BREAD MACHINE, PLUS RISING
COOKING TIME 20 MINUTES   **MAKES** ABOUT 10 GOOD-SIZE ROLLS

1½ cups water
2 tablespoons olive oil
3½ cups white bread flour, plus extra for dusting
1 teaspoon salt

1 teaspoon sugar
1 teaspoon instant dry yeast
1 tablespoon finely chopped fresh rosemary
milk for glazing

1   Pour the water into the bread pan, then add the oil. Sprinkle the flour over, covering the liquid completely. Place the salt and sugar in separate corners of the pan. Make a small indent in the middle of the flour and add the yeast. Close the lid, set the machine to "Dough," and press Start.

2   Meanwhile, grease or flour 2 cookie sheets and set aside. When the dough is ready, remove it from the machine and punch it down on a lightly floured surface, then knead the chopped rosemary evenly into the dough.

3   Divide it into about 10 equal portions. Roll and shape each portion into a ball or oval, then flatten them slightly. Place on the cookie sheets, spacing them well apart. Cover and leave to rise in a warm place about 30 minutes, or until double in size.

4   Preheat the oven to 400°F. Brush the tops of the rolls with milk and dust with flour.

5   Bake about 20 minutes, or until the rolls are golden brown and sound hollow when tapped underneath. Transfer to a wire rack to cool. Serve warm.

panini rolls

PREPARATION TIME 15 MINUTES, PLUS MIXING & KNEADING TIME IN BREAD MACHINE, PLUS RISING
COOKING TIME 15 MINUTES   **MAKES** 12 ROLLS

1 cup water
4 tablespoons extra-virgin olive oil, plus extra
    for glazing
3¼ cups white bread flour

2 teaspoons salt
2 teaspoons sugar
1 package (¼ oz.) instant dry yeast

1   Pour the water into the bread pan, then add the oil. Sprinkle the flour over, covering the liquid
    completely. Place the salt and sugar in separate corners of the pan. Make a small indent in the middle
    of the flour and add the yeast. Close the lid, set the machine to "Dough," and press Start.

2   Meanwhile, grease or flour 2 cookie sheets and set aside. When the dough is ready, remove it from
    the machine and punch it down on a lightly floured surface, then divide it into 12 equal portions.

3   Shape each portion of the dough into a ball and place on the cookie sheets, spacing them well apart.
    Brush with olive oil, cover, and leave to rise in a warm place 20 to 30 minutes, or until double in size.

4   Preheat the oven to 400°F. Using a sharp knife, cut a cross in the top of each roll. Bake about
    15 minutes, or until golden brown. Transfer to a wire rack to cool. Serve warm or cold.

malted country rolls

PREPARATION TIME 15 MINUTES, PLUS MIXING & KNEADING TIME IN BREAD MACHINE, PLUS RISING
COOKING TIME 15 TO 20 MINUTES   **MAKES** 10 TO 12 ROLLS

⅔ cup milk (at room temperature), plus extra
    for glazing
½ cup water
1 tablespoon malt extract
3½ cups whole wheat bread flour

2 teaspoons salt
2 teaspoons soft light brown sugar
2 tablespoons butter, diced
1½ teaspoons instant dry yeast
kibbled or cracked wheat for sprinkling

1   Pour the milk and water into the bread pan, then add the malt extract. Sprinkle the flour over, covering the liquid completely. Place the salt, sugar, and butter in separate corners of the pan. Make a small indent in the middle of the flour and add the yeast. Close the lid, set the machine to "Dough," and press Start.

2   Meanwhile, grease or flour 2 cookie sheets and set aside. When the dough is ready, remove it from the machine and punch it down on a lightly floured surface, then divide it into 10 or 12 equal portions.

3   Shape each portion of dough into a ball or oval and place on the cookie sheets, spacing them well apart. Gently press down on each roll to flatten slightly. Cover and leave to rise in a warm place until double in size.

4   Preheat the oven to 400°F. Lightly brush the rolls with milk and sprinkle with kibbled or cracked wheat. Bake 15 to 20 minutes, or until light brown. Transfer to a wire rack to cool. Serve warm or cold.

golden cheddar knots

PREPARATION TIME 20 MINUTES, PLUS MIXING & KNEADING TIME IN BREAD MACHINE, PLUS RISING
COOKING TIME 15 TO 20 MINUTES   **MAKES** 10 KNOTS

1¼ cups plus 2 tablespoons warm water
   (or according to bread-mix package directions)
1 package (1 lb. 2 oz.) white bread mix
1 teaspoon mustard powder

a few turns of freshly ground black pepper
1 cup finely grated sharp Cheddar cheese
beaten egg or milk for glazing

1   Pour the correct amount of water into the bread pan. Sprinkle the bread mix over, covering the water completely. Sprinkle the mustard powder and black pepper over, then sprinkle ¾ cup of the cheese over. Close the lid, set the machine to "Dough," and press Start.

2   Grease or flour 2 cookie sheets and set aside. When the dough is ready, remove it from the machine and punch it down on a lightly floured surface, then divide it into 10 equal portions.

3   Roll each portion of the dough into a long rope shape and gently tie each one loosely in a single knot. Place on the cookie sheets, spacing them well apart, brush with beaten egg or milk, and sprinkle with the remaining cheese. Cover and leave to rise in a warm place until double in size.

4   Preheat the oven to 400°F. Bake the rolls 15 to 20 minutes, or until risen and golden brown. Transfer to a wire rack to cool. Serve warm or cold.

sun-dried tomato rolls

PREPARATION TIME 20 MINUTES, PLUS MIXING & KNEADING TIME IN BREAD MACHINE, PLUS RISING
COOKING TIME 20 MINUTES   **MAKES** ABOUT 10 GOOD-SIZE ROLLS

1½ cups water
2 tablespoons oil from a jar of sun-dried tomatoes
3½ cups white bread flour, plus extra for dusting
1 teaspoon salt
1 teaspoon sugar

1 teaspoon instant dry yeast
1 cup sun-dried tomatoes in oil, patted dry
   and chopped
milk for glazing

1   Pour the water into the bread pan, then add the oil. Sprinkle the flour over, covering the liquid completely. Place the salt and sugar in separate corners of the pan. Make a small indent in the middle of the flour and add the yeast. Close the lid, set the machine to "Dough," and press Start.

2   Meanwhile, grease or flour 2 cookie sheets and set aside. When the dough is ready, remove it from the machine and punch it down on a lightly floured surface, then knead the chopped tomatoes evenly into the dough.

3   Divide it into about 10 equal portions. Roll and shape each portion into a ball or oval, then flatten slightly. Place on the cookie sheets, spacing them well apart. Cover and leave to rise in a warm place about 30 minutes, or until double in size.

4   Preheat the oven to 400°F. Brush the tops of the rolls with milk and dust with flour. Bake about 20 minutes, or until the rolls are golden brown and sound hollow when tapped underneath. Transfer to a wire rack to cool. Serve warm.

mediterranean olive bread rolls

PREPARATION TIME 20 MINUTES, PLUS MIXING & KNEADING TIME IN BREAD MACHINE, PLUS RISING
COOKING TIME 20 MINUTES   **MAKES** ABOUT 10 GOOD-SIZE ROLLS

1½ cups water
2 tablespoons extra-virgin olive oil, plus extra
    for glazing
3½ cups white bread flour

1 teaspoon salt
1 teaspoon sugar
1 teaspoon instant dry yeast
¾ cup pitted black olives, chopped

1 Pour the water into the bread pan, then add the oil. Sprinkle the flour over, covering the liquid completely. Place the salt and sugar in separate corners of the pan. Make a small indent in the middle of the flour and add the yeast. Close the lid, set the machine to "Dough," and press Start.
2 Meanwhile, grease or flour 2 cookie sheets and set aside. When the dough is ready, remove it from the machine and punch it down on a lightly floured surface, then knead the chopped olives evenly into the dough. Divide it into about 10 equal portions.
3 Roll and shape each portion of dough into a ball or oval, then flatten slightly. Place on the cookie sheets, spacing them well apart. Cover and leave to rise in a warm place about 30 minutes, or until double in size.
4 Preheat the oven to 400°F. Brush the tops of the rolls with olive oil. Bake about 20 minutes, or until the rolls are golden brown and sound hollow when tapped underneath. Transfer to a wire rack to cool. Serve warm.

Variation Knead 1 to 2 tablespoons chopped fresh mixed herbs into the dough with the olives, if desired.

petits pains au lait

PREPARATION TIME 15 MINUTES, PLUS MIXING & KNEADING TIME IN BREAD MACHINE, PLUS RISING
COOKING TIME 15 TO 20 MINUTES **MAKES** 12 ROLLS

1¼ cups milk (at room temperature), plus extra
    for glazing
3¼ cups white bread flour
1½ teaspoons salt

1 tablespoon sugar
4 tablespoons butter, diced
2 teaspoons instant dry yeast

1   Pour the milk into the bread pan. Sprinkle the flour over, covering the milk completely. Place the salt, sugar, and butter in separate corners of the pan. Make a small indent in the middle of the flour and add the yeast. Close the lid, set the machine to "Dough," and press Start.

2   Meanwhile, grease or flour 2 cookie sheets and set aside. When the dough is ready, remove it from the machine and punch it down on a lightly floured surface, then divide it into 12 equal portions.

3   Shape each portion of the dough into a 5-inch-long roll, tapered at each end, and place on the cookie sheets, spacing them well apart. Cover and leave to rise in a warm place 20 to 30 minutes, or until double in size.

4   Preheat the oven to 400°F. Using a sharp knife, slash the top of each roll diagonally several times at regular intervals, then brush them with milk.

5   Bake 15 to 20 minutes, or until golden brown. Transfer to a wire rack to cool. Serve warm or cold.

sesame bagels

PREPARATION TIME 10 MINUTES, PLUS MIXING & KNEADING TIME IN BREAD MACHINE, PLUS 10 MINUTES TO SHAPE BAGELS, PLUS RISING   **COOKING TIME** 30 TO 35 MINUTES   **MAKES** 12 BAGELS

1 cup plus 2 tablespoons water
2 tablespoons sunflower oil
3¼ cups white bread flour
1½ teaspoons salt
1 tablespoon sugar

1 package (¼ oz.) instant dry yeast
1 tablespoon malt extract
milk or water for glazing
about 2 tablespoons sesame seeds for sprinkling

1   Pour the water into the bread pan, then add the oil. Sprinkle the flour over, covering the liquid completely. Place the salt and sugar in separate corners of the pan. Make a small indent in the middle of the flour and add the yeast. Close the lid, set the machine to "Dough," and press Start.

2   Meanwhile, grease 2 cookie sheets and set aside. When the dough is ready, remove it from the machine and punch it down on a lightly floured surface, then divide it into 12 equal portions.

3   Shape each portion of the dough into a ball, then, using a floured wooden spoon handle, make a hole through the middle of each ball. Enlarge the holes by pulling the dough outward a little to form rings. (Bear in mind that the holes will close slightly when the dough is risen and poached.) Place on the cookie sheets, cover, and leave to rise in a warm place until double in size.

4   Preheat the oven to 400°F. Heat a large pan of water to simmering, then stir in the malt extract. Drop each bagel into the water (3 or 4 at a time) and poach about 3 minutes, turning once. Remove from the water and drain well, then return the bagels to the cookie sheets.

5   Brush each bagel with a little milk or water and sprinkle the tops with sesame seeds. Bake about 20 minutes, or until baked through and golden brown. Transfer to a wire rack to cool. Cut in half to serve.

poppy seed knots (pictured left)

PREPARATION TIME 20 MINUTES, PLUS MIXING & KNEADING TIME IN BREAD MACHINE, PLUS RISING

COOKING TIME 15 TO 20 MINUTES   **MAKES** 10 KNOTS

1¼ cups plus 2 tablespoons warm water
   (or according to bread-mix package directions)
1 package (1 lb. 2 oz.) white bread mix

beaten egg or milk for glazing
poppy seeds for sprinkling

1 Pour the correct amount of water into the bread pan. Sprinkle the bread mix over, covering the water completely. Close the lid, set the machine to "Dough," and press Start.

2 Meanwhile, grease or flour 2 cookie sheets and set aside. When the dough is ready, remove it from the machine and punch it down on a lightly floured surface, then divide it into 10 equal portions.

3 Roll each portion of the dough into a long rope shape and gently tie each one loosely in a single knot. Place on the cookie sheets, spacing them well apart, then cover and leave to rise in a warm place until double in size.

4 Preheat the oven to 400°F. Brush the knots with beaten egg or milk and sprinkle with poppy seeds. Bake 15 to 20 minutes, or until risen and golden brown. Transfer to a wire rack to cool. Serve warm or cold.

seeded knots

PREPARATION TIME 20 MINUTES, PLUS MIXING & KNEADING TIME IN BREAD MACHINE, PLUS RISING

COOKING TIME 15 TO 20 MINUTES   **MAKES** 12 KNOTS

1¼ cups plus 3 tablespoons milk (at room temperature)
3½ cups white bread flour
2 teaspoons salt
2 teaspoons sugar

2 tablespoons butter, diced
1 package (¼ oz.) instant dry yeast
caraway seeds, pumpkin seeds, and poppy seeds
   for sprinkling

1 Pour the milk into the bread pan. Sprinkle the flour over, covering the milk completely. Place the salt, sugar, and butter in separate corners of the pan. Make a small indent in the middle of the flour and add the yeast. Close the lid, set the machine to "Dough," and press Start.

2 Meanwhile, grease or flour 2 cookie sheets and set aside. When the dough is ready, remove it from the machine and punch it down on a lightly floured surface, then divide it into 12 equal portions.

3 Roll each portion of the dough into a long rope shape and gently tie each one loosely in a single knot. Place on the cookie sheets, spacing them well apart, then cover and leave to rise in a warm place about 30 minutes, or until double in size.

4 Preheat the oven to 425°F. Lightly brush the knots with a little water and sprinkle 4 rolls with caraway seeds, 4 with pumpkin seeds, and 4 with poppy seeds. Bake 15 to 20 minutes, or until risen and golden brown. Transfer to a wire rack to cool. Serve warm or cold.

CHAPTER 3

flat breads

Flat breads, whether leavened or unleavened, vary in texture, flavor, and shape. They might be crisp or chewy, plain or rich, and most of them are quick and easy to prepare and cook.

Many flat breads provide an ideal accompaniment to numerous dishes; some are great for dipping or mopping up sauces, while others are perfect for filling or wrapping to create a quick meal or snack.

We include a whole variety of tempting flat bread recipes from around the world, ranging from flavorful Spiced Naan Breads and North African Flat Breads, to Sun-Dried Tomato & Olive Focaccia and Pancetta, Pepper & Olive Pizzas.

pita breads

PREPARATION TIME 15 MINUTES, PLUS MIXING & KNEADING TIME IN BREAD MACHINE, PLUS RISING
COOKING TIME 10 MINUTES   **MAKES** 8 PITA BREADS

1 cup water
1 tablespoon olive oil
2½ cups white bread flour

1½ teaspoons salt
1 teaspoon sugar
1 teaspoon instant dry yeast

1   Pour the water into the bread pan, then add the oil. Sprinkle the flour over, covering the liquid completely. Place the salt and sugar in separate corners of the pan. Make a small indent in the middle of the flour and add the yeast. Close the lid, set the machine to "Basic Dough" or "Pizza Dough," and press Start.

2   When the dough is ready, remove it from the machine and punch it down on a lightly floured surface, then divide it into 8 equal portions.

3   Roll out each portion of the dough to form a flat oval, ⅛ to ¼ inch thick and 5½ to 6 inches long. Lay the dough ovals on a floured dish towel, cover, and leave to rise at normal room temperature about 30 minutes.

4   Preheat the oven to 450°F. Put 3 cookie sheets in the oven to heat. Place the pita breads on the hot cookie sheets and bake about 10 minutes, or until puffed and golden brown.

5   Serve warm or wrap in a clean dish towel and leave to cool on a wire rack, then reheat under a broiler when required. To serve, split open, and stuff with your favorite filling.

focaccia breads

PREPARATION TIME 15 MINUTES, PLUS MIXING & KNEADING TIME IN BREAD MACHINE, PLUS RISING
COOKING TIME 20 TO 25 MINUTES   **MAKES** 8 FOCACCIA BREADS

1 cup water
3 tablespoons olive oil, plus extra for drizzling
3¼ cups white bread flour
1 teaspoon salt

1½ teaspoons sugar
1½ teaspoons instant dry yeast
coarse sea salt for sprinkling

1   Pour the water into the bread pan, then add the oil. Sprinkle the flour over, covering the liquid completely. Place the salt and sugar in separate corners of the pan. Make a small indent in the middle of the flour and add the yeast. Close the lid, set the machine to "Basic Dough" or "Pizza Dough," and press Start.

2   Meanwhile, grease or flour 2 cookie sheets and set aside. When the dough is ready, remove it from the machine and punch it down on a lightly floured surface, then divide it into 8 equal portions.

3   Roll each portion of the dough into a ball, then flatten each ball into a circle about 4 inches in diameter, making the edges slightly thicker than the middles. Place on the cookie sheets, cover, and leave to rise in a warm place 30 to 45 minutes, or until slightly risen.

4   Preheat the oven to 400°F. Drizzle a little olive oil over each focaccia, sprinkle with sea salt, and spray with a little water.

5   Bake 20 to 25 minutes, or until risen and golden brown, spraying with a little water again after the first 5 minutes of baking. Transfer to a wire rack to cool. Serve warm or cold, whole, or cut into quarters.

sun-dried tomato & olive focaccia

PREPARATION TIME 20 MINUTES, PLUS MIXING & KNEADING TIME IN BREAD MACHINE, PLUS RISING

COOKING TIME 20 TO 25 MINUTES   **MAKES** 1 LOAF (SERVES 6 TO 8)

1¼ cups water
3 tablespoons olive oil, plus extra for drizzling
3½ cups white bread flour
1 teaspoon salt
1 teaspoon sugar

1 teaspoon instant dry yeast
½ cup sun-dried tomatoes in oil, patted dry
   and chopped
⅓ cup pitted black olives, chopped
coarse sea salt for sprinkling

1   Pour the water into the bread pan, then add the oil. Sprinkle the flour over, covering the liquid completely. Place the salt and sugar in separate corners of the pan. Make a small indent in the middle of the flour and add the yeast. Close the lid, set the machine to "Basic Raisin Dough" (or equivalent), or "Dough," and press Start.

2   Add the tomatoes and olives when the machine makes a sound (beeps) to add extra ingredients during the kneading cycle. (Or add 5 minutes before the end of the kneading cycle.)

3   Meanwhile, grease or flour a cookie sheet and set aside. When the dough is ready, remove it from the machine and punch it down on a lightly floured surface, then roll out the dough to form a large, flat oval about 1 inch thick. Place on the cookie sheet, cover, and leave to rise in a warm place until double in size.

4   Preheat the oven to 400°F. Using your fingertips, make deep dimples all over the surface of the dough. Drizzle with oil and sprinkle with sea salt.

5   Bake 20 to 25 minutes, or until baked through. Transfer to a wire rack to cool. Serve warm or cold in chunks or slices.

north african flat breads

PREPARATION TIME 10 MINUTES, PLUS MIXING & KNEADING TIME IN BREAD MACHINE, PLUS RISING
COOKING TIME 15 TO 20 MINUTES   **MAKES** 8 FLAT BREADS

1 cup water
5 tablespoons olive oil, plus extra for glazing
3½ cups white bread flour, plus extra for dusting

2 teaspoons salt
1½ teaspoons sugar
1½ teaspoons instant dry yeast

1   Pour the water into the bread pan, then add the oil. Sprinkle the flour over, covering the liquid completely. Place the salt and sugar in separate corners of the pan. Make a small indent in the middle of the flour and add the yeast. Close the lid, set the machine to "Basic Dough" or "Pizza Dough," and press Start.

2   Meanwhile, grease or flour 2 cookie sheets and set aside. When the dough is ready, remove it from the machine and punch it down on a lightly floured surface, then divide it into 8 equal portions.

3   Roll out each portion of the dough to make a flat circle about 4 inches in diameter. Place on the cookie sheets, then cover and leave to rise in a warm place about 1 hour, or until slightly risen.

4   Preheat the oven to 450°F. Brush a little oil over the top of each flat bread and dust with a little flour. Bake 15 to 20 minutes, or until risen and golden brown. Serve warm.

moroccan flat breads

PREPARATION TIME 15 MINUTES, PLUS MIXING & KNEADING TIME IN BREAD MACHINE, PLUS RESTING
COOKING TIME 15 TO 20 MINUTES   **MAKES** 4 FLAT BREADS

¾ cup milk (at room temperature)
2 cups white bread flour
1 teaspoon fennel seeds
1 teaspoon salt

2 teaspoons honey
1 teaspoon instant dry yeast
beaten egg for glazing

1   Pour the milk into the bread pan. Sprinkle the flour over, covering the milk completely, then sprinkle the fennel seeds over. Place the salt and honey in separate corners of the pan. Make a small indent in the middle of the flour and add the yeast. Close the lid, set the machine to "Basic Dough" or "Pizza Dough," and press Start.

2   Grease or flour 2 cookie sheets and set aside. When the dough is ready, remove it from the machine and punch it down on a lightly floured surface, then divide it into 4 equal portions.

3   Roll out each portion into a circle about 3½ inches in diameter, and about ¾ inch thick. Place on the cookie sheets, then, using a sharp knife or scissors, cut twelve ½-inch-deep slashes all around the edge of each dough circle at regular intervals. Cover and leave in a warm place 20 minutes.

4   Preheat the oven to 425°F. Brush the tops of the dough circles with beaten egg, then bake 15 to 20 minutes, or until the breads are risen slightly and golden brown. Transfer to a wire rack to cool. Serve whole or cut into quarters.

pancetta, pepper & olive pizzas

PREPARATION TIME 30 MINUTES, PLUS MIXING & KNEADING TIME IN BREAD MACHINE

COOKING TIME 20 TO 25 MINUTES   **MAKES** 2 PIZZAS (EACH PIZZA SERVES 4 TO 6)

FOR THE PIZZA DOUGH
1 cup plus 2 tablespoons water
2 tablespoons olive oil
3¼ cups white bread flour
1 teaspoon salt
2 teaspoons sugar
1½ teaspoons instant dry yeast

FOR THE TOPPING
2 tablespoons olive oil
2 cloves garlic, crushed
1 cup diced smoked pancetta
2 large red bell peppers, seeded and sliced
1 can (15 oz.) crushed tomatoes with herbs, drained
2 tablespoons tomato paste
sea salt and freshly ground black pepper
1 heaped cup pitted black olives
¾ cup freshly grated Parmesan cheese
basil leaves (optional)

1   Make the dough. Pour the water into the bread pan, then add the oil. Sprinkle the flour over, covering the liquid completely. Place the salt and sugar in separate corners of the pan. Make a small indent in the middle of the flour and add the yeast. Close the lid, set the machine to "Basic Dough" or "Pizza Dough," and press Start.

2   Meanwhile, grease or flour 2 cookie sheets and set aside.

3   Prepare the topping. Heat the oil in a skillet. Add the garlic and sauté 30 seconds. Add the pancetta and stir-fry over high heat until it releases its fat and browns lightly; remove from the pan and set aside. Add the peppers to the pan and sauté until just soft. Remove the pan from the heat and add the pancetta to the peppers.

4   When the dough is ready, remove it from the machine and punch it down on a lightly floured surface, then divide it in half. Roll out each piece of dough thinly to form a 12-inch circle. Transfer each pizza crust to a cookie sheet.

5   Preheat the oven to 425°F. Mix together the tomatoes, tomato paste, and seasoning. Spread this mixture evenly over the pizza crusts to within ½ inch of the edge. Spoon the pepper and pancetta mixture evenly over the tomatoes, then scatter the olives over the top. Sprinkle with the Parmesan cheese.

6   Bake 20 to 25 minutes, or until the crust is crisp and the topping is golden. Serve warm, sprinkled with basil leaves, if using.

naan breads

PREPARATION TIME 10 MINUTES, PLUS MIXING & KNEADING TIME IN BREAD MACHINE, PLUS RESTING
COOKING TIME 10 TO 12 MINUTES   **MAKES** 4 GOOD-SIZE NAAN BREADS

½ cup milk (at room temperature)
4 tablespoons plain yogurt (at room temperature)
1 tablespoon sunflower oil
2 cups plus 2 tablespoons white bread flour
1 teaspoon salt

1½ teaspoons sugar
1 teaspoon instant dry yeast
about 3 tablespoons melted ghee or butter
    for brushing

1   Pour the milk into a bowl, add the yogurt and oil, and whisk well. Pour the mixture into the bread pan.
    Sprinkle the flour over, covering the liquid completely. Place the salt and sugar in separate corners
    of the pan. Make a small indent in the middle of the flour and add the yeast. Close the lid, set the
    machine to "Basic Dough" or "Pizza Dough," and press Start.

2   When the dough is ready, remove it from the machine and punch it down on a lightly floured surface,
    then divide it into 4 equal portions.

3   Roll out each portion of the dough to form a flat oval or teardrop shape, about ¼ inch thick and 9 inches
    long; cover and leave 15 minutes.

4   Preheat the oven to 450°F. Put 2 cookie sheets in the oven to heat. Place the naan breads on the hot
    cookie sheets and brush with melted ghee or butter. Bake 10 to 12 minutes, or until puffed. Wrap in a
    clean dish towel and serve warm.

spiced naan breads

PREPARATION TIME 10 MINUTES, PLUS MIXING & KNEADING TIME IN BREAD MACHINE, PLUS RESTING
COOKING TIME 10 TO 12 MINUTES   **MAKES** 4 GOOD-SIZE NAAN BREADS

½ cup milk (at room temperature)
4 tablespoons plain yogurt (at room temperature)
1 tablespoon sunflower oil
2 cups plus 2 tablespoons white bread flour
1½ teaspoons ground coriander
1 teaspoon ground cumin

1 teaspoon cayenne pepper
1 teaspoon salt
1½ teaspoons sugar
1 teaspoon instant dry yeast
about 3 tablespoons melted ghee or butter
   for brushing

1 Pour the milk into a bowl, add the yogurt and oil, and whisk well. Pour the mixture into the bread pan.
   Sprinkle the flour over, covering the liquid completely. Mix the ground spices together, then sprinkle
   the spices over the flour. Place the salt and sugar in separate corners of the pan. Make a small indent
   in the middle of the flour and add the yeast. Close the lid, set the machine to "Basic Dough" or "Pizza
   Dough," and press Start.

2 When the dough is ready, remove it from the machine and punch it down on a lightly floured surface,
   then divide it into 4 equal portions.

3 Roll out each portion of the dough to form a flat oval or teardrop shape, about ¼ inch thick and 9 inches
   long; cover and leave 15 minutes.

4 Preheat the oven to 450°F. Put 2 cookie sheets in the oven to heat. Place the naan breads on the hot
   cookie sheets and brush with melted ghee or butter. Bake 10 to 12 minutes, or until puffed. Wrap in a
   clean dish towel and serve warm.

garlic & coriander naan breads

PREPARATION TIME 10 MINUTES, PLUS MIXING & KNEADING TIME IN BREAD MACHINE, PLUS RESTING

COOKING TIME 10 TO 12 MINUTES   **MAKES** 4 GOOD-SIZE NAAN BREADS

½ cup milk (at room temperature)
4 tablespoons plain yogurt (at room temperature)
1 tablespoon sunflower oil
2 cups plus 2 tablespoons white bread flour
1½ teaspoons ground coriander
1 large clove garlic, crushed
1 teaspoon salt

1½ teaspoons sugar
1 teaspoon instant dry yeast
about 3 tablespoons melted ghee or butter
    for brushing
1 to 2 teaspoons black onion seeds
1 to 2 tablespoons chopped cilantro

1 Pour the milk into a bowl, add the yogurt and oil, and whisk well. Pour the mixture into the bread
   pan. Sprinkle the flour over, covering the liquid completely. Sprinkle the ground coriander and garlic
   over the flour. Place the salt and sugar in separate corners of the pan. Make a small indent in the
   middle of the flour and add the yeast. Close the lid, set the machine to "Basic Dough" or "Pizza
   Dough," and press Start.

2 When the dough is ready, remove it from the machine and punch it down on a lightly floured surface,
   then divide it into 4 equal portions.

3 Roll out each portion of the dough to form a flat oval or teardrop shape, about ¼ inch thick and
   9 inches long; cover and leave 15 minutes.

4 Preheat the oven to 450°F. Put 2 cookie sheets in the oven to heat. Place the naan breads on the hot
   cookie sheets, brush with melted ghee or butter, then sprinkle with onion seeds and chopped cilantro.
   Bake 10 to 12 minutes, or until puffed. Wrap in a clean dish towel and serve warm..

quick breads

Quick breads are quick and easy to make compared to many other types of bread: ingredients are simply mixed together and baked, without the need for prolonged kneading or rising periods, creating a range of delicious sweet and savory breads.

Some quick breads, such as loaf cakes that have been enriched with butter, eggs, or fruit, keep well for several days if wrapped in foil or stored in an airtight container. Others are best served freshly baked and warm from the oven.

We include a wide range of versatile and tasty quick breads to tempt you. Choose from traditional favorites such Golden Gingerbread and Malted Fruit Loaf, or experiment with different flavor combinations, such as Cheese & Date Bread or Celery & Walnut Loaf.

golden gingerbread

PREPARATION TIME 20 MINUTES, PLUS COOLING   **COOKING TIME** 1 HOUR TO 1 HOUR 10 MINUTES
MAKES 1 LOAF (SERVES 8 TO 10)

½ cup packed light soft brown sugar
¾ stick butter
½ cup golden syrup or light corn syrup
1⅔ cups all-purpose flour
a pinch of salt

1 teaspoon baking powder
2 teaspoons ground ginger
1 egg, beaten
⅔ cup milk

1   Remove the kneading blade from the bread pan. Remove the bread pan from the machine, grease and
    line the bottom and sides of the pan, and set aside.

2   Place the sugar, butter, and syrup in a small saucepan and heat slowly, stirring, until melted and
    blended. Remove the pan from the heat and cool the mixture slightly. Sift the flour, salt, baking
    powder, and ginger into a bowl and make a well in the middle. Mix together the egg and milk and
    pour into the well along with the melted mixture. Beat together using a wooden spoon until smooth
    and thoroughly mixed. Pour the batter into the bread pan.

3   Place the bread pan in position in the machine and close the lid. Set the machine to "Bake Only" for
    60 minutes. Press Start.

4   After baking, a fine skewer inserted into the middle of the gingerbread should come out clean.
    If the gingerbread requires more baking, bake on the same setting 5 to 10 minutes longer, or until
    baked through.

5   Remove the bread pan from the machine using oven mitts, then leave to stand 5 minutes, before
    turning the gingerbread out onto a wire rack to cool. Serve warm or cold in slices.

date & walnut loaf

PREPARATION TIME 20 MINUTES, PLUS 15 MINUTES STANDING   **COOKING TIME** 45 TO 55 MINUTES

MAKES 1 LOAF (SERVES 10 TO 12)

1¼ cups pitted dried dates, chopped
⅔ cup boiling water
¾ stick butter, softened
⅓ cup packed soft light brown sugar

1 egg, beaten
1⅔ cups self-rising flour
1 teaspoon baking powder
⅔ cup walnuts, chopped

1   Remove the kneading blade from the bread pan. Remove the bread pan from the machine, grease and line the bottom and sides of the pan, and set aside.

2   Place the dates in a bowl and pour the boiling water over. Stir to mix, then set aside 15 minutes. Cream the butter and sugar together in a separate bowl until pale and fluffy, then gradually beat in the egg. Fold in the flour, baking powder, walnuts, and date mixture, stirring until well mixed. Spoon the batter into the bread pan and smooth the surface.

3   Place the bread pan in position in the machine and close the lid. Set the machine to "Bake Only" for 45 minutes. Press Start.

4   After baking, a fine skewer inserted into the middle of the loaf should come out clean. If the loaf requires more baking, bake on the same setting 5 to 10 minutes longer, or until baked through.

5   Remove the bread pan from the machine using oven mitts, then leave to stand 5 minutes, before turning the loaf out onto a wire rack to cool. Serve warm or cold in slices.

cheese & date bread

PREPARATION TIME 20 MINUTES   **COOKING TIME** 45 TO 55 MINUTES   **MAKES** 1 LOAF (SERVES 8 TO 10)

1⅔ cups self-rising flour
a pinch of salt
4 tablespoons butter, diced
⅔ cup finely grated sharp Cheddar cheese

⅔ cup pitted dried dates, finely chopped
2 eggs
⅔ cup milk

1 Remove the kneading blade from the bread pan. Remove the bread pan from the machine, grease and line the bottom and sides of the pan, and set aside.

2 Sift the flour and salt into a bowl, then lightly cut in the butter until the mixture resembles bread crumbs. Stir in scant ⅔ cup of the cheese and the dates. Beat the eggs and milk together in a separate bowl, then add to the date mixture and mix well to combine. Spoon the mixture into the bread pan and smooth the surface. Sprinkle with the remaining cheese.

3 Place the bread pan in position in the machine and close the lid. Set the machine to "Bake Only" for 45 minutes. Press Start.

4 After baking, a fine skewer inserted into the middle of the bread should come out clean. If the bread requires more baking, bake on the same setting 5 to 10 minutes longer, or until baked through.

5 Remove the bread pan from the machine using oven mitts, then leave to stand 5 minutes, before turning the bread out onto a wire rack to cool. Serve warm or cold in slices.

fruity hazelnut loaf

PREPARATION TIME 20 MINUTES, PLUS 30 MINUTES SOAKING   **COOKING TIME** 1 HOUR TO 1 HOUR 10 MINUTES

MAKES 1 LOAF (SERVES 10 TO 12)

½ cup golden raisins
½ cup ready-to-eat dried apricots, roughly chopped
1⅓ cups bran
1¼ cups milk
¾ cup plus 1½ tablespoons self-rising flour
¼ teaspoon salt
⅔ cup plus 2 tablespoons whole wheat flour

4 tablespoons butter, diced
scant 1 cup hazelnuts, chopped
¾ cup demerara sugar
1 teaspoon apple pie spice
1 teaspoon baking powder
2 eggs, beaten

1 Place the golden raisins, apricots, and bran in a bowl, add the milk, and mix well. Cover and leave to soak 30 minutes. Remove the kneading blade from the bread pan, remove the bread pan from the machine, grease and line the bottom and sides of the pan, and set aside.

2 Sift the white flour and salt into a bowl, stir in the whole wheat flour, then lightly cut in the butter until the mixture resembles bread crumbs. Add the bran batter, hazelnuts, sugar, apple pie spice, baking powder, and eggs, and mix thoroughly. Spoon the batter into the bread pan and smooth the surface.

3 Place the bread pan in position in the machine and close the lid. Set the machine to "Bake Only" for 60 minutes. Press Start.

4 After baking, a fine skewer inserted into the middle of the loaf should come out clean. If the loaf requires more baking, bake on the same setting 5 to 10 minutes longer, or until baked through.

5 Remove the bread pan from the machine using oven mitts, then leave to stand 5 minutes, before turning the loaf out onto a wire rack to cool. Serve warm or cold in slices.

banana & honey loaf

PREPARATION TIME 20 MINUTES   **COOKING TIME** 1 HOUR TO 1 HOUR 10 MINUTES

MAKES 1 LOAF (SERVES 8 TO 10)

1 stick butter, softened
½ cup packed soft light brown sugar
⅓ cup honey
2 eggs, beaten

1⅔ cups self-rising flour
½ teaspoon ground nutmeg or cinnamon
2 large bananas
a squeeze of lemon juice

1   Remove the kneading blade from the bread pan. Remove the bread pan from the machine, grease and line the bottom and sides of the pan, and set aside.

2   Place the butter, sugar, and honey in a bowl and beat together until light and fluffy. Gradually beat in the eggs, then fold in the flour and nutmeg or cinnamon. Peel the bananas and mash the flesh with a little lemon juice. Fold the mashed bananas into the batter until well mixed, then spoon the batter into the bread pan and smooth the surface.

3   Place the bread pan in position in the machine and close the lid. Set the machine to "Bake Only" for 60 minutes. Press Start.

4   After baking, a fine skewer inserted into the middle of the loaf should come out clean. If the loaf requires more baking, bake on the same setting 5 to 10 minutes longer, or until baked through.

5   Remove the bread pan from the machine using oven mitts, then leave to stand 5 minutes, before turning the loaf out onto a wire rack to cool. Serve warm or cold in slices.

malted fruit loaf

PREPARATION TIME 20 MINUTES   **COOKING TIME** 40 TO 50 MINUTES   **MAKES** 1 LOAF (SERVES 10 TO 12)

1⅔ cups self-rising flour
1 teaspoon baking soda
1 teaspoon apple pie spice
3 tablespoons malt extract
2 tablespoons golden syrup or light corn syrup

½ cup milk
1 egg, beaten
¾ cup golden raisins
2 tablespoons honey for glazing

1   Remove the kneading blade from the bread pan. Remove the bread pan from the machine, grease and line the bottom and sides of the pan, and set aside.

2   Sift the flour, baking soda, and apple pie spice into a bowl and set aside. Place the malt extract, syrup, and milk in a saucepan and heat gently until melted and blended, stirring occasionally. Remove from the heat and cool slightly, then beat in the egg.

3   Make a well in the middle of the dry ingredients, then add the melted mixture, mixing well with wooden spoon. Fold in the golden raisins. Spoon the batter into the bread pan and smooth the surface.

4   Place the bread pan in position in the machine and close the lid. Set the machine to "Bake Only" for 40 minutes. Press Start.

5   After baking, a fine skewer inserted into the middle of the loaf should come out clean. If the loaf requires more baking, bake on the same setting 5 to 10 minutes longer, or until baked through.

6   Remove the bread pan from the machine using oven mitts, then leave to stand 5 minutes, before turning the loaf out onto a wire rack to cool. While the loaf is still warm, brush it twice with honey to glaze. Serve warm or cold in slices.

celery & walnut loaf

PREPARATION TIME 25 MINUTES   **COOKING TIME** 45 TO 55 MINUTES   **MAKES** 1 LOAF (SERVES 8 TO 10)

1⅔ cups self-rising flour
1 teaspoon baking powder
4 tablespoons butter, diced
2 sticks celery, finely chopped
½ cup walnuts, finely chopped

⅔ cup finely grated sharp Cheddar cheese
sea salt and freshly ground black pepper
1 egg, beaten
about 4 tablespoons milk

1   Remove the kneading blade from the bread pan. Remove the bread pan from the machine, grease and line the bottom and sides of the pan, and set aside.

2   Sift the flour and baking powder into a bowl, then lightly cut in the butter until the mixture resembles breadcrumbs. Stir in the celery, walnuts, cheese, and seasoning and mix well. Mix in the egg and enough milk to form a soft, but not sticky, dough. Turn the dough onto a lightly floured surface and knead gently until smooth. Shape to fit the bread pan and place it in the pan.

3   Place the bread pan in position in the machine and close the lid. Set the machine to "Bake Only" for 1C minutes. Press Start.

4   After baking, a fine skewer inserted into the middle of the loaf should come out clean. If the loaf requires more baking, bake on the same setting 5 to 10 minutes longer, or until baked through.

5   Remove the bread pan from the machine using oven mitts, then leave to stand 5 minutes, before turning the loaf out onto a wire rack to cool. Serve warm or cold in slices, spread with butter.

fruit & spice loaf

PREPARATION TIME 20 MINUTES   **COOKING TIME** 1 HOUR TO 1 HOUR 10 MINUTES   **MAKES** 1 LOAF (SERVES 10 TO 12)

1⅔ cups self-rising flour
½ teaspoon baking soda
1 tablespoon apple pie spice
½ cup packed soft light brown sugar
⅔ cup golden raisins

⅔ cup raisins
⅔ cup currants
⅔ cup ready-to-eat dried apricots, finely chopped
2 eggs
⅔ cup milk

1   Remove the kneading blade from the bread pan. Remove the bread pan from the machine, grease and line the bottom and sides of the pan, and set aside.

2   Sift the flour, baking soda, and apple pie spice into a bowl. Add the sugar and dried fruit and mix well. Beat the eggs and milk together and add to the fruit mixture. Beat until thoroughly mixed. Spoon the batter into the pan and smooth the surface.

3   Place the bread pan in position in the machine and close the lid. Set the machine to "Bake Only" for 60 minutes. Press Start.

4   After baking, a fine skewer inserted into the middle of the bread should come out clean. If it requires more baking, bake on the same setting 5 to 10 minutes longer, or until baked through.

5   Remove the bread pan from the machine using oven mitts, then leave to stand 5 minutes, before turning the bread out onto a wire rack to cool. Serve warm or cold in slices.

CHAPTER 5

specialty & festive breads

Specialty breads are made from yeasted doughs that are enriched with a combination of other ingredients such as eggs, sugar, butter, dried fruit, or chocolate. Enriched breads, both sweet and savory, vary in texture from soft and airy loaves with a rich and buttery flavor, to deliciously light and flaky, melt-in-the-mouth yeasted pastries, all of which are hard to resist.

Some specialty breads, such as Challah, Stollen, and Panettone, are traditionally baked to celebrate a particular festival or celebration.

We include a delicious selection of enriched, specialty breads from all over the world, among them Orange & Cinnamon Brioche and Pains au Chocolat, as well as tempting delights such as Croissants, Doughnuts, and Coconut Bread. We also include some simpler enriched dough recipes, such as Devonshire Splits, Bath Buns, and Chelsea Buns.

paradise braid

PREPARATION TIME 20 MINUTES, PLUS MIXING & KNEADING TIME IN BREAD MACHINE, PLUS RISING
COOKING TIME 45 TO 50 MINUTES   **MAKES** 1 LOAF (SERVES 10)

⅔ cup milk (at room temperature)
2 extra-large eggs, lightly beaten
3¼ cups white bread flour
½ teaspoon salt
¼ cup sugar
4 tablespoons butter, diced, plus
   2 tablespoons melted

1 package (¼ oz.) instant dry yeast
⅓ cup chopped dried pineapple
⅔ cup chopped ready-to-eat dried pears
⅓ cup blanched almonds, chopped
sifted confectioners' sugar for dusting

1   Whisk the milk and eggs in a bowl and pour into the bread pan. Sprinkle the flour over, covering the liquid completely. Place the salt, sugar, and diced butter in separate corners of the pan. Make a small indent in the middle of the flour and add the yeast. Close the lid, set the machine to "Basic Raisin Dough" (or equivalent), or "Dough," and press Start.

2   Add the pineapple, pears, and almonds when the machine makes a sound (beeps) to add extra ingredients during the kneading cycle. (Or add 5 minutes before the end of the kneading cycle.) Meanwhile, grease a cookie sheet and set aside.

3   When the dough is ready, remove it from the machine and punch it down on a lightly floured surface, then divide it into 3 equal pieces. Roll each piece of dough into a rope shape, about 12 inches long. Braid the dough ropes together, pressing them together at both ends to seal. Place on the cookie sheet. Cover and leave to rise in a warm place until almost double in size.

4   Preheat the oven to 375°F. Bake the braid 45 to 50 minutes, or until risen and golden brown, covering it loosely with foil toward the end of the baking time if the top is browning too quickly.

5   Transfer to a wire rack to cool slightly, then brush with the melted butter and dust with confectioners' sugar. Serve warm or cold in slices.

devonshire splits

PREPARATION TIME 15 MINUTES, PLUS MIXING & KNEADING TIME IN BREAD MACHINE, PLUS RISING
COOKING TIME 15 MINUTES   **MAKES** 10 DEVONSHIRE SPLITS

7½ oz. milk (at room temperature)
2½ cups white bread flour
½ teaspoon salt
3½ tablespoons sugar
3 tablespoons butter, diced

1½ teaspoons instant dry yeast
strawberry or raspberry jam and whippped or
   clotted cream, to serve
sifted confectioners' sugar for dusting

1 Pour the milk into the bread pan. Sprinkle the flour over, covering the milk completely. Place the salt, sugar, and butter in separate corners of the pan. Make a small indent in the middle of the flour and add the yeast. Close the lid, set the machine to "Dough," and press Start.

2 Meanwhile, grease 2 cookie sheets and set aside. When the dough is ready, remove it from the machine and punch it down on a lightly floured surface, then divide it into 10 equal portions and roll each portion into a ball. Place the dough balls on the cookie sheets and flatten them slightly. Cover and leave to rise in a warm place until double in size.

3 Preheat the oven to 425°F. Bake the buns about 15 minutes, or until they feel soft and sound hollow when tapped underneath. Transfer to a wire rack to cool.

4 Split each bun at an angle and fill with jam and cream. Dust with confectioners' sugar just before serving.

pesto-parmesan pull-apart

PREPARATION TIME 20 MINUTES, PLUS MIXING & KNEADING TIME IN BREAD MACHINE, PLUS RISING
COOKING TIME 30 TO 35 MINUTES   **MAKES** 1 LOAF (SERVES 16)

1¼ cups water
3¼ cups white bread flour
1¼ teaspoons salt
1½ teaspoons sugar

1½ teaspoons instant dry yeast
3 tablespoons store-bought green pesto sauce
¼ cup freshly grated Parmesan cheese
beaten egg, for glazing

1   Pour the water into the bread pan. Sprinkle the flour over, covering the water completely. Place the salt and sugar in separate corners of the pan. Make a small indent in the middle of the flour and add the yeast. Close the lid, set the machine to "Dough," and press Start.

2   Meanwhile, grease a deep 9-inch round cake pan and set aside. When the dough is ready, remove it from the machine and punch it down on a lightly floured surface, then roll out the dough to form a 16- x 11-inch rectangle.

3   Spread the pesto sauce evenly over the dough, then sprinkle with the Parmesan cheese. Starting from a long side, roll up the dough fairly tightly, like a jelly roll. Cut into 16 even slices, then place the rolls, cut-side up, in a circular pattern in the cake pan. Cover and leave to rise in a warm place until double in size.

4   Preheat the oven to 400°F. Brush the spirals with beaten egg, then bake 30 to 35 minutes, or until deep golden brown. Cool slightly in the pan, then turn out onto a wire rack to cool completely. Pull the rolls apart to serve and serve warm or cold.

cheese & herb tear "n" share

PREPARATION TIME 15 MINUTES, PLUS MIXING & KNEADING TIME IN BREAD MACHINE, PLUS RISING

COOKING TIME 40 MINUTES   **MAKES** 1 LOAF (SERVES 12)

1¼ cups plus 2 tablespoons warm water
   (or according to bread-mix package directions)
1 package (1 lb. 2 oz.) white bread mix
7 tablespoons butter, melted
1 extra-large egg, lightly beaten

2 tablespoons freshly grated Parmesan cheese
2 cloves garlic, crushed
½ teaspoon salt
¼ teaspoon freshly ground black pepper
2 teaspoons dried herbes de Provence

1   Pour the correct amount of water into the bread pan. Sprinkle the bread mix over, covering the water completely. Close the lid, set the machine to "Dough," and press Start.

2   Meanwhile, grease a deep 8-inch round cake pan and set aside. When the dough is ready, remove it from the machine and punch it down on a lightly floured surface, then divide it into 12 equal portions and roll each portion into a ball.

3   Combine the melted butter, egg, Parmesan cheese, garlic, salt, black pepper, and dried herbs in a small bowl. Dip the dough balls into the butter mixture, coating them liberally all over, then arrange them in a single layer in the cake pan. Drizzle any remaining butter mixture over. Cover and leave to rise in a warm place about 45 minutes, or until double in size.

4   Preheat the oven to 375°F. Bake the loaf about 40 minutes, or until golden brown. Turn out and cool on a wire rack. Pull the rolls apart to serve and serve warm or cold.

coconut bread

PREPARATION TIME 10 MINUTES   **COOKING TIME** VARIES ACCORDING TO BREAD MACHINE

MAKES 1 LOAF (SERVES 10 TO 12)

1¼ cups plus 2 tablespoons milk
   (at room temperature)
1 teaspoon vanilla extract
3¼ cups white bread flour
½ cup shredded coconut

1½ teaspoons salt
1 tablespoon sugar
1 tablespoon butter, diced
1½ teaspoons instant dry yeast

1   Pour the milk into the bread pan and add the vanilla extract. Sprinkle the flour over, covering the milk completely, then sprinkle the coconut over. Place the salt, sugar, and butter in separate corners of the pan. Make a small indent in the middle of the flour and add the yeast.

2   Close the lid and set the machine to "Sweet" or "Basic White"/"Normal" (or equivalent), then select the loaf size and crust type. Press Start.

3   After baking, remove the bread pan from the machine and turn the loaf out onto a wire rack to cool. Serve in slices.

monkey bread

PREPARATION TIME 25 MINUTES, PLUS OVERNIGHT SOAKING, PLUS MIXING & KNEADING TIME IN
BREAD MACHINE, PLUS RISING   **COOKING TIME** 40 MINUTES   **MAKES** 1 LOAF (SERVES 16)

⅔ cup golden raisins
4 tablespoons brandy
¾ cup milk (at room temperature)
3½ tablespoons water
1 extra-large egg, lightly beaten
3¼ cups white bread flour
½ teaspoon salt

2 teaspoons sugar
1 package (¼ oz.) instant dry yeast
scant 1 cup walnuts, finely chopped
1½ teaspoons apple pie spice
⅔ cup packed soft light brown sugar
¾ stick butter, melted

1   Place the golden raisins in a bowl, add the brandy, and stir; leave to soak overnight.
2   Pour the milk and water into a bowl, add the egg, and whisk well. Pour the mixture into the bread
    pan. Sprinkle the flour over, covering the liquid completely. Place the salt and sugar in separate
    corners of the pan. Make a small indent in the middle of the flour and add the yeast. Close the lid,
    set the machine to "Dough," and press Start.
3   Meanwhile, grease a 9-inch loose-bottomed springform pan fitted with a tube base, or a ring mold,
    and set aside. Mix the walnuts, apple pie spice, and brown sugar in a bowl and set aside. When the
    dough is ready, remove it from the machine and punch it down on a lightly floured surface, then divide
    it into 32 pieces and roll each piece into a ball.
4   Dip each ball of dough into the melted butter, then roll in the walnut mixture, covering completely.
    Place half the balls in the pan, spacing them slightly apart. Spoon the soaked golden raisins and any
    remaining walnut mixture over. Top with the rest of the dough balls and drizzle any remaining butter
    over. Cover and leave to rise in a warm place about 45 minutes, or until double in size.
5   Preheat the oven to 375°F. Bake the bread about 40 minutes, or until risen and golden brown. Cool in
    the pan 10 minutes, then invert onto a serving plate. Pull the rolls apart to serve and serve warm or cold.

challah

PREPARATION TIME 20 MINUTES, PLUS MIXING & KNEADING TIME IN BREAD MACHINE, PLUS RISING
COOKING TIME 35 TO 40 MINUTES   **MAKES** 1 LOAF (SERVES 10)

⅔ cup water
5 tablespoons olive oil
2 eggs, lightly beaten
3½ cups white bread flour
1½ teaspoons salt

1 tablespoon sugar
1 package (¼ oz.) instant dry yeast
beaten egg for glazing
sesame or poppy seeds for sprinkling

1 Pour the water into a bowl, add the oil and eggs, and whisk well. Pour the mixture into the bread pan. Sprinkle the flour over, covering the liquid completely. Place the salt and sugar in separate corners of the pan. Make a small indent in the middle of the flour and add the yeast. Close the lid, set the machine to "Dough," and press Start.

2 Meanwhile, grease a large cookie sheet and set aside. When the dough is ready, remove it from the machine and punch it down on a lightly floured surface, then divide it into 4 equal portions.

3 Roll each portion of the dough into a rope about 16 inches long. Place the ropes of dough side by side and pinch them together at one end. Starting from the right, make a braid, lifting the first rope over the second and the third rope over the fourth, then placing the fourth rope between the first and second ropes. Repeat and continue, to form a braid, pinching the ends together when you have finished. Tuck the ends under at each end of the braid and place the braid on the cookie sheet. Cover and leave to rise in a warm place until double in size.

4 Preheat the oven to 425°F. Brush the dough with beaten egg and sprinkle with sesame or poppy seeds. Bake 15 minutes, then reduce the oven temperature to 375°F and bake 20 to 25 minutes longer, or until risen and golden brown. Transfer to a wire rack to cool. Serve in slices or wedges.

orange & cinnamon brioche

PREPARATION TIME 25 MINUTES, PLUS MIXING & KNEADING TIME IN BREAD MACHINE, PLUS RISING
COOKING TIME 30 MINUTES   **MAKES** 1 LOAF (SERVES 12 TO 14)

1¼ sticks butter
3 extra-large eggs, lightly beaten
2 tablespoons milk
1 tablespoon finely grated orange zest
3¼ cups white bread flour

1 teaspoon ground cinnamon
1 teaspoon salt
¼ cup sugar
1 package (¼ oz.) instant dry yeast
beaten egg yolk for glazing

1   Melt 5 tablespoons of the butter. Whisk the melted butter, eggs, milk, and orange zest together in
    a bowl, then pour into the bread pan. Sprinkle the flour over, covering the liquid completely, then
    sprinkle the cinnamon over. Place the salt, sugar, and remaining butter in separate corners of the pan.
    Make a small indent in the middle of the flour and add the yeast. Close the lid, set the machine to
    "Dough," and press Start.

2   Grease a 1¾-quart brioche pan and set aside. When the dough is ready, remove it from the machine
    and punch it down on a lightly floured surface, then cut one-quarter from the dough and set aside.
    Knead the remaining piece of dough, shape it into a large ball, and place it in the pan.

3   Shape the reserved piece of dough into a pear shape. Make a hollow in the middle of the large ball of
    dough and place the thinner end of the pear-shaped piece of dough into the hollow. Cover and leave
    to rise in a warm place until the dough nearly reaches the top of the pan.

4   Preheat the oven to 400°F. Brush the brioche with beaten egg yolk, then bake about 30 minutes, or
    until risen and golden. Turn out and cool on a wire rack. Serve warm or cold.

bath buns

PREPARATION TIME 15 MINUTES, PLUS MIXING & KNEADING TIME IN BREAD MACHINE, PLUS RISING
COOKING TIME 20 MINUTES   **MAKES** ABOUT 16 BUNS

⅔ cup milk (at room temperature)
2 eggs, lightly beaten
4 tablespoons butter, melted
3½ cups white bread flour
1 teaspoon salt
¼ cup sugar

2 teaspoons instant dry yeast
1 cup golden raisins
⅓ cup chopped mixed candied peel
beaten egg, for glazing
1 ounce (about 4 tablespoons) sugar cubes,
    coarsely crushed

1 Whisk the milk, eggs, and melted butter in a bowl, then pour into the bread pan. Sprinkle the flour
   over, covering the liquid completely. Place the salt and sugar in separate corners of the pan. Make a
   small indent in the middle of the flour and add the yeast. Close the lid and set the machine to "Basic
   Raisin Dough" (or equivalent), or "Dough," and press Start.

2 Add the golden raisins and mixed peel when the machine makes a sound (beeps) to add extra
   ingredients during the kneading cycle. (Or add 5 minutes before the end of the kneading cycle.)
   Meanwhile, grease 2 cookie sheets and set aside.

3 When the dough is ready, remove it from the machine and punch it down on a lightly floured surface,
   then divide it into about 16 equal portions. Knead each portion of dough into a ball and place on the
   cookie sheets. Flatten each ball slightly. Cover and leave to rise in a warm place until double in size.

4 Preheat the oven to 375°F. Brush the tops of the buns with beaten egg and sprinkle with the crushed
   sugar cubes. Bake about 20 minutes, or until risen and golden brown. Transfer to a wire rack to cool
   and serve warm or cold on their own or split and spread with butter.

lardy cake

PREPARATION TIME 25 MINUTES, PLUS MIXING & KNEADING TIME IN BREAD MACHINE, PLUS RISING
COOKING TIME 30 MINUTES   **MAKES** 1 CAKE (SERVES 10 TO 12)

1¼ cups water
3¼ cups white bread flour
1 teaspoon salt
2 tablespoons sugar, plus 1 tablespoon
    for the glaze
5 ounces lard
1½ teaspoons instant dry yeast

½ cup packed soft light brown sugar
½ cup currants
½ cup golden raisins
⅓ cup chopped mixed candied peel
1 teaspoon apple pie spice
1 tablespoon boiling water

1   Pour the water into the bread pan. Sprinkle the flour over, covering the water completely. Place
the salt, sugar, and 1 tablespoon of the lard in separate corners of the pan. Make a small indent in
the middle of the flour and add the yeast. Close the lid, set the machine to "Dough," and press Start.
Meanwhile, grease a 10- x 8-inch shallow roasting pan and set aside.

2   When the dough is ready, remove it from the machine and punch it down on a floured surface, then
roll out the dough to form a rectangle about ¼ inch thick. With a short side of the rectangle nearest
to you, dot the top two-thirds of the dough with flakes of one-third of the remaining lard. Sprinkle
one-third each of the brown sugar, dried fruits, mixed peel, and apple pie spice over. Fold the bottom
third of the dough up over the middle third, then fold the top third down over the middle third to form
an envelope. Seal the edges with a rolling pin. Give the dough a quarter turn so the folded side is
to the left.

3   Repeat this whole procedure, rolling, filling, and folding the dough, twice more, using the remaining
lard, brown sugar, dried fruits, mixed peel, and apple pie spice. Fold, seal, and turn as before. Roll out
the dough to fit in the pan and place it inside. Cover and leave to rise in a warm place 1 to 1½ hours,
or until almost double in size.

4   Preheat the oven to 400°F. Score the top of the dough in a crisscross pattern, then bake about
30 minutes, or until risen and golden brown.

5   Dissolve the remaining 1 tablespoon sugar in the boiling water, then brush this glaze over the top of
the warm cake. Leave to cool in the pan a few minutes, then turn out, and serve warm or cold, cut
into slices or squares.

panettone

PREPARATION TIME 25 MINUTES, PLUS MIXING & KNEADING TIME IN BREAD MACHINE, PLUS RISING

COOKING TIME 45 TO 50 MINUTES   **MAKES** 1 LOAF (SERVES 8 TO 10)

3 extra-large eggs, lightly beaten
3 tablespoons milk
2⅔ cups white bread flour
½ teaspoon salt
¼ cup superfine sugar
1 stick butter, soft

2 teaspoons instant dry yeast
⅔ cup golden raisins
⅓ cup chopped mixed candied peel
finely grated zest of 1 small lemon
1 tablespoon butter, melted, for glazing

1   Whisk the eggs and milk in a bowl. Pour the mixture into the bread pan. Sprinkle the flour over, covering the liquid completely. Place the salt and sugar in separate corners of the pan. Dot the soft butter over the surface, then make a small indent in the middle of the flour and add the yeast. Close the lid, set the machine to "Basic Raisin Dough" (or equivalent), or "Dough," and press Start.

2   Add the golden raisins, mixed peel, and lemon zest when the machine makes a sound (beeps) to add extra ingredients during the kneading cycle. (Or add 5 minutes before the end of the kneading cycle.)

3   Grease and line a deep 7-inch round cake pan. Tie a double layer of wax paper around the outside of the pan, with string, making the collar about 3 inches above the rim; set aside.

4   When the dough is ready, remove it from the machine and punch it down on a lightly floured surface, then shape the dough into a ball. Place in the pan and cut a cross in the top. Cover and leave to rise in a warm place until double in size.

5   Preheat the oven to 400°F. Brush the top of the dough with the melted butter. Bake 15 minutes, then reduce the oven temperature to 350°F and bake 30 to 35 minutes longer, or until the top is golden brown and crisp. Turn out and cool on a wire rack.

hot cross buns

PREPARATION TIME 20 MINUTES, PLUS MIXING & KNEADING TIME IN BREAD MACHINE, PLUS RISING

COOKING TIME 15 TO 20 MINUTES   **MAKES** 12 TO 14 BUNS

1 cup milk (at room temperature)
1 extra-large egg, lightly beaten
3¼ cups white bread flour
1 teaspoon apple pie spice
1 teaspoon ground cinnamon
1 teaspoon grated nutmeg
1 teaspoon salt
6 tablespoons sugar

4 tablespoons butter, diced
1½ teaspoons instant dry yeast
finely grated zest of 1 lemon
½ cup golden raisins
2 tablespoons chopped mixed candied peel
3 ounces piecrust dough
3 tablespoons water

1   Pour the milk into a bowl, add the egg, and whisk well. Pour the mixture into the bread pan. Sprinkle the flour over, covering the liquid completely, then sprinkle the ground spices over. Place the salt, 2 tablespoons of the sugar, and the butter in separate corners of the pan. Make a small indent in the middle of the flour and add the yeast. Close the lid, set the machine to "Basic Raisin Dough" (or equivalent), or "Dough", and press Start.

2   Add the lemon zest, golden raisins, and mixed peel when the machine makes a sound (beeps) to add extra ingredients during the kneading cycle. (Or add 5 minutes before the end of the kneading cycle.) Meanwhile, grease 2 cookie sheets and set aside.

3   When the dough is ready, remove it from the machine and punch it down on a lightly floured surface, then divide it into 12 or 14 equal portions.

4   Knead each portion into a ball and place on the cookie sheets. Flatten each ball slightly. Roll out the piecrust dough on a lightly floured surface and cut into narrow strips. Brush the buns with a little water and top each one with a dough cross. Cover and leave to rise in a warm place until double in size.

5   Preheat the oven to 375°F. Bake the buns 15 to 20 minutes, or until golden. Transfer to a wire rack.

6   Meanwhile, make the glaze. Dissolve the remaining sugar in a saucepan with the water. Heat gently, stirring until the sugar has dissolved, then bring to a boil and boil rapidly 2 minutes. As soon as the buns come out of the oven, brush them twice with the sugar glaze. Leave to cool and serve warm or cold.

croissants

PREPARATION TIME 35 MINUTES, PLUS MIXING & KNEADING TIME IN BREAD MACHINE, PLUS RISING
COOKING TIME 15 TO 20 MINUTES **MAKES** 12 CROISSANTS

1¼ cups milk (at room temperature)
3½ cups white bread flour
1 teaspoon salt
2 tablespoons sugar

2½ sticks butter (at room temperature)
1 package (¼ oz.) instant dry yeast
beaten egg for glazing

1 Pour the milk into the bread pan. Sprinkle the flour over, covering the milk completely. Place the salt, sugar, and 4 tablespoons of the butter in separate corners of the pan. Make a small indent in the middle of the flour and add the yeast. Close the lid and set the machine to "Dough," and press Start.

2 Meanwhile, grease 2 cookie sheets and set aside. When the dough is ready, remove it from the machine and punch it down on a lightly floured surface, then roll it out to form a 14- x 7-inch rectangle.

3 Flatten the remaining butter into a block about ¾ inch thick. With a short side of the dough rectangle nearest to you, place the butter on top of the dough so it covers the top two-thirds of the rectangle. Fold the bottom third of the dough over the middle third, then fold the top buttered third down over the top of the middle third to form an envelope. Seal the edges with a rolling pin.

4 Give the dough a quarter turn so the folded side is to the left. Roll into a rectangle as before, then fold the bottom third up and the top third down and seal the edges, as before. Wrap in wax paper and chill in the refrigerator 20 minutes. Repeat the rolling, folding, and chilling twice more, turning the dough 90 degrees each time before rolling.

5 Roll out the dough on a lightly floured surface to form a 21- x 14-inch rectangle and cut into 12 equal triangles. Roll up each triangle, starting from the long side and ending with the point of the triangle. Bend the ends of each croissant around to make a crescent or half-moon shape. Place on the cookie sheets. Cover and leave to rise in a warm place about 30 minutes, or until almost double in size.

6 Preheat the oven to 425°F. Lightly brush the croissants with beaten egg, then bake 15 to 20 minutes, or until crisp and golden brown. Serve warm.

chelsea buns

PREPARATION TIME 20 MINUTES, PLUS MIXING & KNEADING TIME IN BREAD MACHINE, PLUS RISING

COOKING TIME 25 TO 30 MINUTES   **MAKES** 12 BUNS

7 tablespoons milk (at room temperature)

1 extra-large egg, lightly beaten

1½ cups white bread flour

½ teaspoon salt

2 tablespoons sugar

4 tablespoons butter, diced

1 teaspoon instant dry yeast

½ cup mixed raisins and currants

⅓ cup golden raisins

¼ cup packed soft light brown sugar

1½ teaspoons ground cinnamon

2 tablespoons clear honey for glazing

1   Whisk the milk and egg together in a bowl and pour into the bread pan. Sprinkle the flour over, covering the liquid completely. Place the salt, sugar, and 2 tablespoons of the butter in separate corners of the pan. Make a small indent in the middle of the flour and add the yeast. Close the lid, set the machine to "Dough," and press Start.

2   Grease a 7-inch square cake pan and set aside. When the dough is ready, remove it from the machine and punch it down on a lightly floured surface, then roll it out into a 12- x 9-inch rectangle.

3   Melt the remaining butter and brush it over the dough. Combine the dried fruit, brown sugar, and cinnamon and sprinkle evenly over the dough, leaving a 1-inch border around the edges.

4   Starting from a long side, roll up the dough fairly tightly, like a jelly roll. Cut into 12 even slices and place, cut-sides up, in the pan. Cover and leave to rise in a warm place until double in size.

5   Preheat the oven to 375°F. Bake the buns 25 to 30 minutes, or until risen and golden brown. Remove from the oven and brush twice with honey while still hot. Cool slightly, then turn out onto a wire rack. Serve warm or cold.

easter bread ring

PREPARATION TIME 25 MINUTES, PLUS MIXING & KNEADING TIME IN BREAD MACHINE, PLUS RISING

COOKING TIME 20 TO 25 MINUTES   **MAKES** 1 RING (SERVES 10 TO 12)

7 tablespoons milk (at room temperature),
    plus extra for glazing
1 extra-large egg, lightly beaten
1⅔ cups white bread flour
½ teaspoon salt
2 tablespoons sugar
4 tablespoons butter, diced
1 teaspoon instant dry yeast

½ cup golden raisins
½ cup ready-to-eat dried apricots, chopped
¼ cup packed soft light brown sugar
1½ teaspoons apple pie spice
1 cup confectioners' sugar, sifted
about 4 teaspoons water
¼ cup toasted slivered almonds

1   Whisk the milk and egg in a bowl and pour into the pan. Sprinkle the flour over, covering the liquid
    completely. Place the salt, sugar, and 2 tablespoons of the butter in separate corners of the pan.
    Make a small indent in the middle of the flour and add the yeast. Close the lid, set the machine to
    "Dough," and press Start.

2   Grease a cookie sheet and set aside. When the dough is ready, remove it from the machine and punch
    it down on a lightly floured surface, then roll out the dough into an 18- x 12-inch rectangle. Melt the
    remaining butter and brush it over the dough. Sprinkle with the fruit, brown sugar, and spice.

3   Starting from a long side, roll up the dough like a jelly roll, then shape it into a circle, seam-side down.
    Brush the ends with milk and press them together to seal. Place the dough ring on the cookie sheet.

4   Using a sharp knife, make cuts two-thirds of the way through the dough at 1½-inch intervals, twisting
    the slices outward at an angle so they overlap slightly. Cover and leave to rise in a warm place until
    double in size.

5   Preheat the oven to 400°F. Bake 20 to 25 minutes, or until golden brown. Transfer the ring to a wire
    rack to cool. Mix the confectioners' sugar with the water to make
    a thin glacé frosting and drizzle it over the warm
    baked ring. Sprinkle with the almonds.
    Serve warm or cold in slices.

doughnuts

PREPARATION TIME 20 MINUTES, PLUS MIXING & KNEADING TIME IN BREAD MACHINE, PLUS RISING
COOKING TIME 25 MINUTES   **MAKES** 16 DOUGHNUTS

¾ cup milk (at room temperature)
2 extra-large eggs, lightly beaten
3½ cups white bread flour
1 teaspoon salt
¾ cup plus 2 tablespoons sugar

2 tablespoons butter, diced
1½ teaspoons instant dry yeast
⅓ cup strawberry or raspberry jam
sunflower oil for deep-frying
1½ teaspoons ground cinnamon

1   Pour the milk into a bowl, add the eggs, and whisk well. Pour the mixture into the bread pan. Sprinkle the flour over, covering the liquid completely. Place the salt, half the sugar, and the butter in separate corners of the pan. Make a small indent in the middle of the flour and add the yeast. Close the lid, set the machine to "Dough," and press Start.

2   Meanwhile, oil 2 cookie sheets and set aside. When the dough is ready, remove it from the machine and punch it down on a lightly floured surface, then divide it into 16 equal portions.

3   Shape each portion of dough into a ball, then flatten each one to about ½ inch thick. Place 1 heaped teaspoon of jam into the middle of each flattened ball and gather the edges of the dough up and over the jam, enclosing it completely, then pinch the edges firmly together to seal and roll into a ball. Place on the cookie sheets, cover, and leave to rise in a warm place about 30 minutes, or until almost double in size.

4   Heat some oil in a deep-fat fryer to 325°F and fry the doughnuts in batches in the hot oil about 6 minutes, or until golden all over, turning once. Remove the doughnuts from the fryer using a slotted spoon and drain on paper towels.

5   Combine the remaining sugar and the cinnamon in a bowl and toss the doughnuts in the sugar mixture, coating them all over. Serve immediately.

pains au chocolat

PREPARATION TIME 35 MINUTES, PLUS MIXING & KNEADING TIME IN BREAD MACHINE, PLUS RISING

COOKING TIME 15 TO 20 MINUTES   **MAKES** 12 PAINS AU CHOCOLAT

1¼ cups milk (at room temperature)
3½ cups white bread flour
1 teaspoon salt
2 tablespoons sugar
2½ sticks butter (at room temperature)

1 package (¼ oz.) instant dry yeast
6 ounces semisweet or milk chocolate,
    finely chopped
beaten egg, for glazing

1   Pour the milk into the bread pan. Sprinkle the flour over, covering the milk completely. Place the salt, sugar, and 4 tablespoons of the butter in separate corners of the pan. Make a small indent in the middle of the flour and add the yeast. Close the lid, set the machine to "Dough," and press Start.

2   Grease 2 cookie sheets and set aside. When the dough is ready, remove it from the machine and punch it down on a lightly floured surface, then roll out the dough to form a rectangle about 21 x 14 inches.

3   Flatten the remaining butter into a block about ¾ inch thick. With a short side of the dough rectangle nearest to you, place the butter on top of the dough so it covers the top two-thirds of the rectangle. Fold the bottom third of the dough over the middle third, then fold the top buttered third down over the top of the middle third to form an envelope. Seal the edges with a rolling pin.

4   Give the dough a quarter turn so the folded side is to the left. Roll into a rectangle as before, then fold the bottom third up and the top third down and seal the edges, as before. Wrap in wax paper and chill in the refrigerator 20 minutes. Repeat the rolling, folding, and chilling twice more, turning the dough 90 degrees each time, before rolling.

5   Roll out the dough on a lightly floured surface to form a 21- x 14-inch rectangle and cut into 12 equal rectangles. Place 1 tablespoon of the chopped chocolate along one end of each rectangle. Roll up each rectangle to make a flattish cylinder shape, enclosing the chocolate completely. Place seam-side down on the cookie sheets. Cover and leave to rise in a warm place until almost double in size.

6   Preheat the oven to 400°F. Lightly brush the pastries with beaten egg, then bake 15 to 20 minutes until crisp and golden brown. Serve warm.

danish apple braid

PREPARATION TIME 25 MINUTES, PLUS MIXING & KNEADING TIME IN BREAD MACHINE, PLUS RISING

COOKING TIME 20 TO 25 MINUTES   **MAKES** 1 LOAF (SERVES 8)

7 tablespoons milk (at room temperature)

1 extra-large egg, lightly beaten

1¾ cups white bread flour

½ teaspoon salt

2 tablespoons butter, diced

¼ cup sugar

1 teaspoon instant dry yeast

5 ounces store-bought almond paste,
    coarsely grated

1 large or 2 small cooking apples, peeled, cored,
    and thinly sliced

1 teaspoon ground cinnamon

beaten egg for glazing

¾ cup confectioners' sugar, sifted

1 tablespoon toasted slivered almonds or chopped
    pistachio nuts, to decorate

1   Whisk the milk and egg in a bowl and pour into the bread pan. Sprinkle the flour over, covering the liquid completely. Place the salt, butter, and 2 tablespoons of the sugar in separate corners of the pan. Make a small indent in the middle of the flour and add the yeast. Close the lid, set the machine to "Dough," and press Start.

2   Grease a cookie sheet and set aside. When the dough is ready, remove it from the machine and punch it down on a lightly floured surface, then roll it out to form a 12- x 10-inch rectangle. Place the almond paste evenly down the middle third (lengthwise) of the dough, about 2½ to 3 inches wide.

3   Toss the apple slices with the remaining sugar and the cinnamon, then spoon this mixture evenly over the almond paste. On the longest sides of the dough, make diagonal cuts up to the filling at 1-inch intervals. Braid the strips of dough over the filling, pressing lightly to seal. Tuck the ends under to seal at both ends of the braid. Place the braid on the cookie sheet, then cover and leave to rise in a warm place until double in size.

4   Preheat the oven to 400°F. Lightly brush the braid with beaten egg, then bake 20 to 25 minutes until risen and golden. Transfer to a wire rack to cool.

5   Blend the confectioners' sugar with a little water to make a thin frosting. Drizzle the frosting over the warm braid, then sprinkle with almonds or pistachio nuts. Serve warm or cold in slices.

stollen

PREPARATION TIME 25 MINUTES, PLUS MIXING & KNEADING TIME IN BREAD MACHINE, PLUS RISING

COOKING TIME 40 MINUTES   **MAKES** 1 LOAF (SERVES 10 TO 12)

⅔ cup milk (at room temperature)
1 extra-large egg, lightly beaten
2½ cups white bread flour
1 teaspoon apple pie spice
½ teaspoon salt
2 tablespoons sugar
3 tablespoons butter, diced

1½ teaspoons instant dry yeast
1 cup mixed dried fruit
½ cup blanched almonds, finely chopped
finely grated zest of 1 lemon
6 ounces store-bought almond paste
confectioners' sugar and ground cinnamon
    for dusting

1   Whisk the milk and egg in a bowl and pour into the bread pan. Sprinkle the flour over, covering the
    liquid completely, then sprinkle the apple pie spice over. Place the salt, sugar, and butter in separate
    corners of the pan. Make a small indent in the middle of the flour and add the yeast. Close the lid, set
    the machine to "Basic Raisin Dough" (or equivalent), or "Dough," and press Start.

2   Mix together the dried fruit, almonds, and lemon zest and set aside. Add the dried fruit mixture when
    the machine makes a sound (beeps) to add extra ingredients during the kneading cycle. (Or add 5 minutes
    before the end of the kneading cycle.)

3   Grease a cookie sheet and set aside. When the dough is ready, remove it from the machine and punch
    it down on a lightly floured surface, then roll it out into a rectangle about 9 x 6 inches in size.

4   Roll the almond paste into a long rope shape, just a little shorter than the length of the rectangle,
    and place the almond-paste log along the middle of the dough. Fold the dough over almost in half to
    enclose it and press the edges together to seal. Transfer to the cookie sheet, cover, and leave to rise
    in a warm place until double in size.

5   Preheat the oven to 350°F. Bake the loaf about 40 minutes, or until deep golden brown. Transfer to a
    wire rack to cool. Dust with a mixture of sifted confectioners' sugar and cinnamon. Serve in slices.

apple & cinnamon pull-apart

PREPARATION TIME 25 MINUTES, PLUS MIXING & KNEADING TIME IN BREAD MACHINE, PLUS RISING

COOKING TIME 25 TO 30 MINUTES   **MAKES** 1 LOAF (SERVES 12)

⅔ cup milk (at room temperature)

½ cup water

1 extra-large egg, lightly beaten

3¼ cups white bread flour

1 teaspoon salt

2 tablespoons sugar

2 teaspoons instant dry yeast

¾ cup packed soft light brown sugar

1½ teaspoons ground cinnamon

3 eating apples, peeled, cored, and thinly sliced

4 tablespoons heavy cream

2 tablespoons butter, diced

¼ cup hazelnuts, finely chopped

1   Whisk the milk, water, and egg in a bowl and pour into the bread pan. Sprinkle the flour over, covering the liquid completely. Place the salt and sugar in separate corners of the pan. Make a small indent in the middle of the flour and add the yeast. Close the lid, set the machine to "Dough," and press Start.

2   Grease a 9-inch loose-bottomed springform pan fitted with a tube base, or a ring mould, and set aside. When the dough is ready, remove it from the machine and punch it down on a lightly floured surface, then roll out the dough to form a 16- x 8-inch rectangle.

3   Combine ¼ cup of the brown sugar and the cinnamon, then add the apple slices and toss to mix well. Spoon the mixture evenly over the dough, leaving an ½-inch border around the edges. Starting from a long side, roll up the dough fairly tightly, like a jelly roll. Cut into 12 even slices, then place the slices upright but at an angle, so they rest on each other, in the pan. Cover and leave to rise in a warm place 1½ to 2 hours, or until double in size.

4   Preheat the oven to 375°F. Bake 25 to 30 minutes, or until risen and golden brown. Cool slightly in the pan, then turn out onto a wire rack.

5   Meanwhile, place the remaining brown sugar, the cream, and butter in a small pan and heat gently, stirring, until the sugar dissolves. Bring gently to a boil, then simmer, uncovered, about 4 minutes, or until the mixture thickens slightly.

6   Brush the hot pull-apart with the caramel mixture, then sprinkle with the hazelnuts. Pull the rolls apart to serve and serve warm or cold.

loaf cakes & baked goods

Delicious, moist loaf cakes and baked goods are perfect for serving with a cup of coffee or tea as a tasty afternoon snack, although most can be enjoyed as a treat at any time of the day.

Loaf cakes are generally easy to make and those enriched with butter or eggs will keep well for a few days if wrapped or stored in an airtight container. Baked goods, such as muffins, should be eaten freshly baked or toasted.

Choose from iced delights such as Lemon-Blueberry Loaf Cake and Frosted Orange Loaf Cake, or enjoy munching on Marbled Chocolate Loaf Cake and Hawaiian Fruit Loaf. For a more traditional and hard-to-resist treat, split and toast Teacake Fingers and serve them hot, spread with melting butter.

frosted raisin loaf cake

PREPARATION TIME 20 MINUTES, PLUS OVERNIGHT SOAKING

COOKING TIME 1¼ HOURS TO 1 HOUR 25 MINUTES   **MAKES** 1 LOAF (SERVES 10 TO 12)

1¼ cups raisins
⅔ cup golden raisins
1¼ cups strong hot tea, strained
1¼ cups packed soft light brown sugar
2¼ cups self-rising flour

1½ teaspoons apple pie spice
1 egg, beaten
1½ cups confectioners' sugar, sifted
about 5 to 6 teaspoons orange juice

1   Place the raisins and golden raisins in a large bowl, pour over the hot tea, and stir to mix. Cover and
leave to soak overnight.

2   The next day, remove the kneading blade from the bread pan. Remove the bread pan from the
machine, grease and line the bottom and sides of the pan, and set aside. Stir the brown sugar into
the fruit mixture, then sift in the flour and apple pie spice. Add the egg and mix throroughly with a
wooden spoon. Spoon the mixture into the bread pan and smooth the surface.

3   Place the bread pan in position in the machine and close the lid. Set the machine to "Bake Only" for
75 minutes. Press Start.

4   After baking, a fine skewer inserted into the middle of the loaf should come out clean. If the loaf
requires more baking, bake on the same setting 5 to 10 minutes longer, or until baked through.

5   Remove the bread pan from the machine using oven mitts, then leave to stand 5 minutes, before
turning the loaf out onto a wire rack to cool completely.

6   Combine the confectioners' sugar with enough orange juice to make a thick, smooth frosting. Spread
the frosting evenly over the top of the cold loaf. Leave to set. Serve in slices.

malted golden raisin loaf cake

PREPARATION TIME 10 MINUTES **COOKING TIME** VARIES ACCORDING TO BREAD MACHINE

MAKES 1 LOAF (SERVES 10)

1½ cups water
3 tablespoons malt extract
3½ cups white bread flour
1 tablespoon skim milk powder
1½ teaspoons salt

2 teaspoons sugar
2 tablespoons butter, diced
1 teaspoon instant dry yeast
⅔ cup golden raisins

1 Pour the water into the bread pan, then add the malt extract. Sprinkle the flour over, covering the liquid completely. Sprinkle the milk powder over the flour. Place the salt, sugar, and butter in separate corners of the pan. Make a small indent in the middle of the flour and add the yeast.

2 Close the lid, set the machine to "Basic White"/"Normal," with "Raisin," if available (or equivalent), then select the loaf size and crust type. Press Start.

3 Add the golden raisins when the machine makes a sound (beeps) to add extra ingredients during the kneading cycle. (Or add 5 minutes before the end of the kneading cycle.)

4 After baking, remove the bread pan from the machine, then turn the cake out onto a wire rack to cool. Serve in slices.

Variation Use raisins, sweetened dried cranberries, or chopped ready-to-eat dried apricots or pears in place of golden raisins.

banana-chip muesli loaf cake

PREPARATION TIME 15 MINUTES   **COOKING TIME** 1 TO 1¼ HOURS   **MAKES** 1 LOAF (SERVES 10)

1½ sticks butter, softened
¾ cup packed soft light brown sugar
3 eggs, beaten
1¼ cups self-rising flour

⅓ cup muesli (of your choice),
  such as Swiss-style muesli
½ cup banana chips
sifted confectioners' sugar for decorating (optional)

1   Remove the kneading blade from the bread pan. Remove the bread pan from the machine, grease and line the bottom and sides of the pan, and set aside.

2   Cream the butter and brown sugar together in a bowl until light and fluffy, then gradually beat in the eggs. Sift the flour into the bowl, then fold the flour into the creamed mixture together with the muesli and banana chips, mixing well. Spoon the batter into the bread pan and smooth the surface.

3   Place the bread pan in position in the machine and close the lid. Set the machine to "Bake Only" for 60 minutes. Press Start.

4   After baking, a fine skewer inserted into the middle of the cake should come out clean. If the cake requires more baking, bake on the same setting 10 to 15 minutes longer, or until baked through.

5   Remove the bread pan from the machine using oven mitts, then leave to stand 10 minutes, before turning the cake out onto a wire rack to cool. Dust with sifted confectioners' sugar, if desired, and serve warm or cold in slices.

frosted orange loaf cake

PREPARATION TIME 15 MINUTES   **COOKING TIME** 1 HOUR TO 1 HOUR 10 MINUTES   **MAKES** 1 LOAF (SERVES 10)

FOR THE LOAF CAKE
1 stick butter, soft
¼ cup packed soft light brown sugar
2 eggs, beaten
1 cup self-rising flour, sifted
heaped 1 cup whole wheat flour
1½ teaspoons baking powder
1½ teaspoons ground ginger
½ teaspoon salt

8 tablespoons orange marmalade
about 1 tablespoon milk

FOR THE FROSTING
¾ stick butter, soft
1 teaspoon finely grated orange zest
1½ cups confectioners' sugar, sifted
2 teaspoons orange juice
thinly pared orange zest, to decorate (optional)

1   Remove the kneading blade from the bread pan. Remove the bread pan from the machine, grease and line the bottom and sides of the pan, and set aside.

2   For the loaf cake, cream the butter and brown sugar together in a bowl until light and fluffy, then gradually beat in the eggs. Sift over the flours, baking powder, ground ginger, and salt into the creamed mixture, mixing well and adding any bran left behind in the sifter. Fold in the marmalade and enough milk to make a fairly soft consistency. Spoon the batter into the bread pan and smooth the surface.

3   Place the bread pan in position in the machine and close the lid. Set the machine to "Bake Only" for 60 minutes. Press Start.

4   After baking, a fine skewer inserted into the middle of the loaf should come out clean. If the loaf requires more baking, bake on the same setting 5 to 10 minutes longer, or until baked through.

5   Remove the bread pan from the machine using oven mitts. Leave to stand 10 minutes, before turning the loaf out onto a wire rack to cool completely.

6   Meanwhile, make the frosting. Cream the butter in a bowl until pale and fluffy, then beat in the grated orange zest. Gradually stir in the confectioners' sugar and orange juice, mixing to make a soft frosting. Spread the frosting over the top of the cold loaf and sprinkle with the pared orange zest, if desired. Serve in slices.

lemon-blueberry loaf cake

PREPARATION TIME 15 MINUTES   **COOKING TIME** 1 TO 1¼ HOURS   **MAKES** 1 LOAF (SERVES 10)

1⅔ cups self-rising flour
1 stick butter, diced
½ cup plus 1 tablespoon sugar
⅓ cup finely ground blanched almonds or hazelnuts
finely grated zest and juice of 1 lemon

2 eggs, beaten
4 tablespoons milk
1½ cups fresh blueberries, rinsed and dried
½ cup confectioners' sugar, sifted

1 Remove the kneading blade from the bread pan. Remove the bread pan from the machine, grease and line the bottom and sides of the pan, and set aside.

2 Sift the flour into a bowl, then lightly cut in the butter. Stir in the sugar, nuts, and lemon zest, then beat in the eggs and milk, mixing well. Fold in the blueberries. Spoon the batter into the bread pan and smooth the surface.

3 Place the bread pan in position in the machine and close the lid. Set the machine to "Bake Only" for 60 minutes. Press Start.

4 After baking, a fine skewer inserted into the middle of the loaf should come out clean. If the loaf requires more baking, bake on the same setting 10 to 15 minutes longer, or until baked through.

5 Remove the pan from the machine using oven mitts. Leave to stand 10 minutes, before turning the loaf out onto a wire rack to cool completely.

6 Meanwhile, make the frosting. Combine the confectioners' sugar with 1 to 2 teaspoons lemon juice to make a fairly thin frosting. Drizzle the frosting over the cold loaf. Serve in slices.

marbled chocolate loaf cake

PREPARATION TIME 25 MINUTES   **COOKING TIME** 55 TO 65 MINUTES   **MAKES** 1 CAKE (SERVES 10)

1½ sticks butter, soft
¾ cup packed soft light brown sugar
3 eggs, beaten
1⅔ cups all-purpose flour
2½ teaspoons baking powder

2 ripe bananas, peeled and mashed with lemon juice
¼ cup unsweetened cocoa powder, plus extra for dusting
2 teaspoons milk
½ teaspoon ground ginger
sifted confectioners' sugar for dusting

1   Remove the kneading blade from the bread pan. Remove the bread pan from the machine, grease and line the bottom and sides of the pan, and set aside.

2   Cream the butter and brown sugar together in a bowl. Gradually beat in the eggs. Sift the flour and baking powder over and fold in, mixing well. Fold in the bananas.

3   Place half the batter in a separate bowl. Sift the cocoa powder over, add the milk, and fold together. Stir the ground ginger into the plain banana batter. Place alternate spoonfuls of each batter into the bread pan, then gently swirl a sharp knife or skewer through the mixture to create a marbled effect.

4   Place the bread pan in position in the machine and close the lid. Set the machine to "Bake Only" for 55 minutes. Press Start.

5   After baking, a fine skewer inserted into the middle of the loaf should come out clean. If the loaf requires more baking, bake on the same setting 5 to 10 minutes longer, or until baked through.

6   Remove the bread pan from the machine and leave to stand 10 minutes, then turn the loaf out onto a wire rack to cool. Dust with sifted confectioners' sugar, if desired, and serve warm or cold.

apricot & walnut loaf cake

PREPARATION TIME 20 MINUTES   **COOKING TIME** 1 TO 1¼ HOURS   **MAKES** 1 LOAF (SERVES 10)

2 cups all-purpose flour
2½ teaspoons baking powder
1½ teaspoons apple pie spice
¾ stick butter, diced
½ cup packed soft light brown sugar

1¼ cups ready-to-eat dried apricots, chopped
⅔ cup golden raisins
⅔ cup walnuts, chopped
7 ounces milk
1 egg, beaten

1   Remove the kneading blade from the bread pan. Remove the bread pan from the machine, grease and line the bottom and sides of the pan, and set aside.

2   Sift the flour, baking powder, and apple pie spice into a bowl, then lightly cut in the butter. Stir in the sugar, apricots, golden raisins, and walnuts. Gradually beat in the milk and egg until well mixed. Spoon the batter into the bread pan and smooth the surface.

3   Place the bread pan in position in the machine and close the lid. Set the machine to "Bake Only" for 60 minutes. Press Start.

4   After baking, a fine skewer inserted into the middle of the loaf should come out clean. If the loaf requires more baking, bake on the same setting 10 to 15 minutes longer, or until baked through.

5   Remove the bread pan from the machine using oven mitts, then leave to stand 5 minutes before turning the loaf out onto a wire rack to cool. Serve warm or cold in slices.

Variations Use raisins or dried blueberries in place of golden raisins. Use hazelnuts or pecans in place of walnuts.

hawaiian fruit loaf

PREPARATION TIME 15 MINUTES, PLUS OVERNIGHT SOAKING   **COOKING TIME** 1 TO 1¼ HOURS
MAKES 1 LOAF (SERVES 10)

1¼ cups mixed ready-to-eat dried tropical fruit,
   chopped
¾ cup strong hot tea, strained
heaped 1¾ cups whole wheat flour
1 tablespoon baking powder
1½ teaspoons apple pie spice

¾ cup packed soft light brown sugar
finely grated zest of 1 orange
¼ cup shredded coconut
1 egg, beaten
4 tablespoons milk
sifted confectioners' sugar, to decorate

1   Put the mixed fruit in a large bowl, pour the hot tea over, stir to mix, and leave to soak overnight.
2   The next day, remove the kneading blade from the bread pan. Remove the bread pan from the
    machine, grease and line the bottom and sides of the pan, and set aside.
3   Combine the flour, baking powder, apple pie spice, brown sugar, orange zest, and coconut in a bowl.
    Add to the soaked fruits, together with the egg and milk, and mix thoroughly. Spoon the batter into
    the bread pan and smooth the surface.
4   Place the bread pan in position in the machine and close the lid. Set the machine to "Bake Only" for
    60 minutes. Press Start.
5   After baking, a fine skewer inserted into the middle of the bread should come out clean. If the loaf
    requires more baking, bake on the same setting 10 to 15 minutes longer, or until baked through.
6   Remove the bread pan from the machine using oven mitts.
    Leave to stand 5 minutes, before turning the loaf out onto a
    wire rack to cool. Dust with sifted confectioners' sugar.
    Serve warm or cold in slices.

teacakes

PREPARATION TIME 15 MINUTES, PLUS MIXING & KNEADING TIME IN BREAD MACHINE, PLUS RISING
COOKING TIME 20 TO 25 MINUTES   **MAKES** 8 TEACAKES

1¼ cups milk (at room temperature), plus extra
    for glazing
3¼ cups white bread flour
1¼ teaspoons salt

2 tablespoons sugar
2 tablespoons butter, diced
1½ teaspoons instant dry yeast
⅔ cup currants

1   Pour the milk into the bread pan. Sprinkle the flour over, covering the milk completely. Place the salt, sugar, and butter in separate corners of the pan. Make a small indent in the middle of the flour and add the yeast. Close the lid, set the machine to "Basic Raisin Dough" (or equivalent), or "Dough", and press Start.

2   Add the currants when the machine makes a sound (beeps) to add extra ingredients during the kneading cycle. (Or add 5 minutes before the end of the kneading cycle.) Meanwhile, grease 2 cookie sheets and set aside.

3   When the dough is ready, remove it from the machine and punch it down on a lightly floured surface, then divide it into 8 equal portions. Roll and shape each portion of dough into a round flattened ball and prick each one twice on top with a fork. Place on the cookie sheets, cover, and leave to rise in a warm place until double in size.

Preheat the oven to 400°F. Brush the teacakes with a little milk, then bake 20 to 25 minutes, or until risen and golden brown. Transfer to a wire rack to cool. To serve, split each teacake in half, toast lightly, and spread with butter or jam.

teacake fingers

PREPARATION TIME 15 MINUTES, PLUS MIXING & KNEADING TIME IN BREAD MACHINE, PLUS RISING

COOKING TIME 20 MINUTES   **MAKES** 12 TEACAKE FINGERS

⅔ cup milk (at room temperature)
¾ cup warm water (or according to bread-mix
    package directions)
1 package (1 lb. 2 oz.) white bread mix
2 tablespoons sugar

1 teaspoon apple pie spice
2 tablespoons butter, diced
⅔ cup golden raisins
⅓ cup chopped mixed candied peel
beaten egg for glazing

1   Pour the milk and correct amount of water into the bread pan. Sprinkle the bread mix over, covering the liquid completely. Sprinkle the sugar and apple pie spice over, then dot the butter over the surface. Close the lid, set the machine to "Basic Raisin Dough" (or equivalent), or "Dough," and press Start.

2   Add the golden raisins and mixed peel when the machine makes a sound (beeps) to add extra ingredients during the kneading cycle. (Or add 5 minutes before the end of the kneading cycle.)

3   Meanwhile, grease or flour 2 cookie sheets and set aside. When the dough is ready, remove it from the machine and punch it down on a lightly floured surface, then divide it into 12 equal portions.

4   Roll and shape each portion of dough into a long roll or finger shape and place on the cookie sheets. Cover and leave to rise in a warm place about 30 minutes, or until double in size.

5   Preheat the oven to 375°F. Brush the teacakes with beaten egg, then bake about 20 minutes, or until risen and golden brown. Transfer to a wire rack to cool. Serve split, lightly toasted, and spread with butter.

english muffins

PREPARATION TIME 20 MINUTES, PLUS MIXING & KNEADING TIME IN BREAD MACHINE, PLUS RISING
COOKING TIME 35 MINUTES   **MAKES** 8 TO 10 MUFFINS

⅔ cup milk (at room temperature)
½ cup water
4 tablespoons butter, melted
3¼ cups white bread flour

1½ teaspoons salt
1 teaspoon sugar
1½ teaspoons instant dry yeast
sunflower oil for greasing

1 Pour the milk and water into a bowl, add the melted butter, and whisk well. Pour the mixture into the bread pan. Sprinkle the flour over, covering the liquid completely. Place the salt and sugar in separate corners of the pan. Make a small indent in the middle of the flour and add the yeast. Close the lid, set the machine to "Dough," and press Start.

2 Meanwhile, generously flour a large cookie sheet and set aside. When the dough is ready, remove it from the machine and punch it down on a lightly floured surface, then divide the dough into 8 to 10 equal portions.

3 Shape each portion of dough into a circle with straight sides, ½ to ¾ inch thick. Place on the cookie sheet, cover, and leave to rise in a warm place 30 to 40 minutes, or until springy to the touch.

4 Brush a griddle or large, heavy-bottomed skillet with a little oil and heat until warm. Carefully transfer 3 to 4 muffins onto the griddle and cook over medium heat 8 to 10 minutes, or until golden brown underneath. Turn them over and cook the other side about 8 minutes, or until golden brown.

5 Remove the muffins from the pan and wrap them in a clean dish towel, if serving warm. Otherwise, transfer them to a wire rack to cool. Cook the remaining muffins in batches.

6 To serve, split the muffins open and serve with butter. If serving from cold, toast the muffins on both sides, then split and spread with butter.

english whole wheat muffins

PREPARATION TIME 20 MINUTES, PLUS MIXING & KNEADING TIME IN BREAD MACHINE, PLUS RISING
COOKING TIME 35 MINUTES   **MAKES** 8 TO 10 MUFFINS

1½ cups milk (at room temperature)
1⅔ cups white bread flour
heaped 1¾ cups whole wheat flour
1½ teaspoons salt

1 teaspoon sugar
1 tablespoon butter, diced
1½ teaspoons instant dry yeast
sunflower oil for greasing

1 Pour the milk into the bread pan. Sprinkle each flour over in turn, covering the milk completely. Place the salt, sugar, and butter in separate corners of the pan. Make a small indent in the middle of the flour and add the yeast. Close the lid, set the machine to "Dough," and press Start.

2 Meanwhile, generously flour a large cookie sheet and set aside. When the dough is ready, remove it from the machine and punch it down on a lightly floured surface, then divide the dough into 8 to 10 equal portions.

3 Shape each portion of dough into a circle with straight sides, ½ to ¾ inch thick. Place on the cookie sheet, cover, and leave to rise in a warm place about 30 minutes, or until almost double in size.

4 Brush a griddle or large, heavy-bottomed skillet with a little oil and heat until warm. Carefully transfer 3 or 4 muffins onto the griddle and cook over medium heat 7 to 10 minutes, or until golden brown underneath. Turn them over and cook the other side about 7 minutes, or until golden brown.

5 Remove the muffins from the pan and wrap them in a clean dish towel, if serving warm. Otherwise, transfer them to a wire rack to cool. Cook the remaining muffins in batches.

6 To serve, split the muffins open and serve with butter. If serving from cold, toast the muffins on both sides, then split and spread with butter.

loaf cakes & baked goods

gluten-free breads

For those with a sensitivity to gluten, this chapter is an invaluable source of creative and tasty recipes.

Gluten-free breads, by the very nature of the ingredients used to create them, tend to be slightly different in texture and flavor from traditional breads, but are just as appealing and delicious. They have a slightly more crumbly and closer, but light, texture, and many are enjoyed at their best when served warm and freshly baked.

There is an excellent selection of gluten-free recipes in this chapter, including Gluten-Free White Bread, Gluten-Free Brown Bread, Fresh Herb Bread, and Italian Tomato Bread, as well as sweet recipes, such as Spiced Honey Loaf Cake and Apricot & Cranberry Loaf Cake.

gluten-free white bread (pictured right)

PREPARATION TIME 10 MINUTES   **COOKING TIME** VARIES ACCORDING TO BREAD MACHINE

MAKES 1 LOAF (SERVES 10 TO 12)

1¼ cups plus 2 tablespoons milk
  (at room temperature)
4 tablespoons sunflower oil
2 eggs, lightly beaten

3¼ cups gluten-free white baking flour
2 tablespoons sugar
1 teaspoon salt
1 package (¼ oz.) instant dry yeast

1   Pour the milk into a bowl, add the oil and eggs, and whisk together well to mix. Pour the mixture into the bread pan. Sprinkle the flour over, covering the liquid completely. Sprinkle the sugar evenly over the flour, then add the salt. Make a small indent in the middle of the flour and add the yeast.

2   Close the lid and set the machine to "Rapid Bake" (or equivalent), then select the loaf size and crust type. Press Start.

3   A couple of minutes after mixing has begun, lift the lid of the machine briefly and scrape down the sides of the pan with a plastic spatula for even mixing. Close the lid once again.

4   After baking, remove the bread pan from the machine and turn the loaf out onto a wire rack to cool. Serve in slices.

gluten-free whole wheat bread

PREPARATION TIME 10 MINUTES   **COOKING TIME** VARIES ACCORDING TO BREAD MACHINE

MAKES 1 LOAF (SERVES 10 TO 12)

1¼ cups plus 2 tablespoons milk
  (at room temperature)
4 tablespoons sunflower oil
2 eggs, lightly beaten

3½ cups gluten-free whole wheat flour
2 tablespoons sugar
1 teaspoon salt
1 package (¼ oz.) instant dry yeast

1   Pour the milk into a bowl, add the oil and eggs, and whisk together well to mix. Pour the mixture into the bread pan. Sprinkle the flour over, covering the liquid completely. Sprinkle the sugar evenly over the flour, then add the salt. Make a small indent in the middle of the flour and add the yeast.

2   Close the lid and set the machine to "Rapid Bake" (or equivalent), then select the loaf size and crust type. Press Start.

3   A couple of minutes after mixing has begun, lift the lid of the machine briefly and scrape down the sides of the pan with a plastic spatula for even mixing. Close the lid once again.

4   After baking, remove the bread pan from the machine and turn the loaf out onto a wire rack to cool. Serve in slices.

fresh herb bread

PREPARATION TIME 15 MINUTES   **COOKING TIME** VARIES ACCORDING TO BREAD MACHINE

MAKES 1 LOAF (SERVES 10 TO 12)

2¾ cups plus 2 tablespoons gluten-free white
    baking flour
⅓ cup gram (chickpea) flour
9 ounces water
2 eggs, beaten
4 tablespoons olive oil

4 tablespoons chopped fresh mixed herbs, such as
    parsley, basil, oregano, and chives
⅓ cup freshly grated Parmesan cheese
1 tablespoon sugar
1½ teaspoons salt
2½ teaspoons instant dry yeast

1 Combine the flours and set aside. Pour the water into a bowl, add the eggs, oil, and chopped herbs, and whisk together well to mix. Pour the mixture into the bread pan. Sprinkle the cheese over, then sprinkle the mixed flours over, covering the liquid completely. Sprinkle the sugar evenly over the flour, then add the salt. Make a small indent in the middle of the flour and add the yeast.

2 Close the lid and set the machine to "Rapid Bake" (or equivalent), then select the loaf size and crust type. Press Start.

3 A couple of minutes after mixing has begun, lift the lid of the machine briefly and scrape down the sides of the pan with a plastic spatula for even mixing. Close the lid once again.

4 After baking, remove the bread pan from the machine and turn the loaf out onto a wire rack to cool. Serve in slices.

mixed seed loaf

PREPARATION TIME 10 MINUTES   **COOKING TIME** VARIES ACCORDING TO BREAD MACHINE

MAKES 1 LOAF (SERVES 10 TO 12)

1¼ cups plus 2 tablespoons milk
 (at room temperature)
4 tablespoons sunflower oil
2 eggs, lightly beaten
3¼ cups gluten-free white baking flour

5 tablespoons mixed seeds, such as sunflower,
 pumpkin, caraway, poppy seeds, and linseeds
2 tablespoons sugar
1 teaspoon salt
1 package (¼ oz.) instant dry yeast

1   Pour the milk into a bowl, add the oil and eggs, and whisk together well to mix. Pour the mixture into
    the bread pan. Sprinkle the flour over, covering the liquid completely. Sprinkle the mixed seeds evenly
    over the flour. Sprinkle the sugar over, then add the salt. Make a small indent in the middle of the
    flour and add the yeast.
2   Close the lid and set the machine to "Rapid Bake" (or equivalent), then select the loaf size and crust
    type. Press Start.
3   A couple of minutes after mixing has begun, lift the lid of the machine briefly and scrape down the
    sides of the pan with a plastic spatula for even mixing. Close the lid once again.
4   After baking, remove the bread pan from the machine and turn the loaf out onto a wire rack to cool.
    Serve in slices.

italian tomato bread

PREPARATION TIME 15 MINUTES   **COOKING TIME** VARIES ACCORDING TO BREAD MACHINE
MAKES 1 LOAF (SERVES 10 TO 12)

1¼ cups plus 2 tablespoons milk
   (at room temperature)
2 tablespoons oil from a jar of sun-dried tomatoes
2 tablespoons olive oil
2 eggs, lightly beaten
⅓ cup freshly grated Parmesan cheese

¾ cup sun-dried tomatoes in oil, patted dry
   and chopped
3½ cups gluten-free whole wheat flour
2 tablespoons sugar
1 teaspoon salt
1 package (¼ oz.) instant dry yeast

1   Pour the milk into a bowl, add the oils and eggs, and whisk together well to mix. Pour the mixture into the bread pan. Sprinkle the cheese over the milk mixture, followed by the tomatoes. Sprinkle the flour over, covering the liquid, cheese, and tomatoes completely. Sprinkle the sugar evenly over the flour, then add the salt. Make a small indent in the middle of the flour and add the yeast.

2   Close the lid and set the machine to "Rapid Bake" (or equivalent), then select the loaf size and crust type. Press Start.

3   A couple of minutes after mixing has begun, lift the lid of the machine briefly and scrape down the sides of the pan with a plastic spatula for even mixing. Close the lid once again.

4   After baking, remove the bread pan from the machine and turn the loaf out onto a wire rack to cool. Serve in slices.

cheese & mustard bread

PREPARATION TIME 15 MINUTES   **COOKING TIME** VARIES ACCORDING TO BREAD MACHINE

MAKES 1 LOAF (SERVES 10 TO 12)

2⅔ cups plus 2 tablespoons gluten-free
   white baking flour
⅓ cup gram (chickpea) flour
1¼ cups water
2 eggs, beaten
4 tablespoons olive oil

3 tablespoons gluten-free wholegrain mustard
⅔ cup finely grated sharp Cheddar cheese
1 tablespoon sugar
1½ teaspoons salt
2½ teaspoons instant dry yeast

1   Combine the flours and set aside. Place the water in a bowl, add the eggs, oil, and mustard, and whisk together well to mix. Pour the mixture into the bread pan. Sprinkle the cheese over, then sprinkle the flours over, covering the liquid and cheese completely. Sprinkle the sugar evenly over the flour, then add the salt. Make a small indent in the middle of the flour and add the yeast.

2   Close the lid and set the machine to "Rapid Bake" (or equivalent), then select the loaf size and crust type. Press Start.

3   A couple of minutes after mixing has begun, lift the lid of the machine briefly and scrape down the sides of the pan with a plastic spatula for even mixing. Close the lid once again.

4   After baking, remove the bread pan from the machine and turn the loaf out onto a wire rack to cool. Serve in slices.

herbed olive bread

PREPARATION TIME 15 MINUTES   **COOKING TIME** VARIES ACCORDING TO BREAD MACHINE

MAKES 1 LOAF (SERVES 10 TO 12)

1¼ cups plus 2 tablespoons milk
   (at room temperature)
4 tablespoons olive oil
2 eggs, lightly beaten
2 teaspoons dried Italian herb seasoning
½ cup freshly grated Parmesan cheese

½ cup pitted black olives, chopped
3 cups gluten-free whole wheat flour
2 tablespoons sugar
1 teaspoon salt
1 package (¼ oz.) instant dry yeast

1 Pour the milk into a bowl, add the oil, eggs, and dried herbs, and whisk together well to mix. Pour the mixture into the bread pan. Sprinkle the cheese over the milk, followed by the olives. Sprinkle the flour over, covering the liquid, cheese, and olives completely. Sprinkle the sugar evenly over the flour, then add the salt. Make a small indent in the middle of the flour and add the yeast.

2 Close the lid and set the machine to "Rapid Bake" (or equivalent), then select the loaf size and crust type. Press Start.

3 A couple of minutes after mixing has begun, lift the lid of the machine briefly and scrape down the sides of the pan with a plastic spatula for even mixing. Close the lid once again.

4 After baking, remove the bread pan from the machine and turn the loaf out onto a wire rack to cool. Serve in slices.

spiced honey loaf cake

PREPARATION TIME 20 MINUTES **COOKING TIME** 50 TO 60 MINUTES **MAKES** 1 LOAF (SERVES 8)

½ cup packed soft light brown sugar
¾ stick butter
½ cup honey
1⅔ cups gluten-free white flour
a pinch of salt

1 teaspoon gluten-free baking powder
2 teaspoons apple pie spice
1 egg, beaten
⅔ cup milk

1   Remove the kneading blade from the bread pan. Remove the bread pan from the machine, grease and line the bottom and sides of the pan, and set aside.

2   Place the sugar, butter, and honey in a saucepan and heat slowly until melted, stirring. Remove the pan from the heat and cool slightly. Sift the flour, salt, baking powder, and apple pie spice into a bowl and make a well in the middle. Mix together the egg and milk and pour into the middle of the dry ingredients together with the melted honey mixture. Beat together using a wooden spoon until smooth and thoroughly mixed. Pour the batter into the bread pan.

3   Place the bread pan in position in the machine and close the lid. Set the machine to "Bake Only" for 50 minutes. Press Start.

4   After baking, a fine skewer inserted into the middle of the loaf should come out clean. If the loaf requires more baking, bake on the same setting 5 to 10 minutes longer, or until baked through.

5   Remove the bread pan from the machine using oven mitts, then leave to stand 5 minutes, before turning the loaf out onto a wire rack to cool. Serve warm or cold in slices.

Variations Use golden syrup in place of honey. Use ground ginger or cinnamon in place of apple pie spice.

sticky spiced loaf cake

PREPARATION TIME 20 MINUTES, PLUS COOLING   **COOKING TIME** 50 TO 60 MINUTES   **MAKES** 1 LOAF (SERVES 8)

½ cup packed soft light brown sugar
¾ stick butter
⅓ cup golden syrup or light corn syrup
2½ tablespoons molasses
1½ cups gluten-free white flour
a pinch of salt

1 teaspoon gluten-free baking powder
2 teaspoons apple pie spice
1 teaspoon ground ginger
1 egg, beaten
⅔ cup milk

1   Remove the kneading blade from the bread pan. Remove the bread pan from the machine, grease and line the bottom and sides of the pan, and set aside.

2   Place the sugar, butter, syrup, and molasses in a saucepan and heat slowly until melted, stirring. Remove the pan from the heat and cool slightly. Sift the flour, salt, baking powder, and ground spices into a bowl and make a well in the middle. Mix together the egg and milk and pour into the middle of the dry ingredients together with the melted syrup mixture. Beat together using a wooden spoon until smooth and thoroughly mixed. Pour the batter into the bread pan.

3   Place the bread pan in position in the machine and close the lid. Set the machine to "Bake Only" for 50 minutes. Press Start.

4   After baking, a fine skewer inserted into the middle of the loaf should come out clean. If the loaf requires more baking, bake on the same setting 5 to 10 minutes longer, or until baked through.

5   Remove the bread pan from the machine using oven mitts, then leave to stand 5 minutes, before turning the loaf out onto a wire rack to cool. Serve warm or cold in slices.

Variation Use ground cinnamon in place of ginger.

apricot & cranberry loaf cake

PREPARATION TIME 20 MINUTES   **COOKING TIME** 1 TO 1¼ HOURS   **MAKES** 1 LOAF (SERVES 10)

1½ cups gluten-free white flour
2 teaspoons gluten-free baking powder
1 stick butter, diced
½ cup packed soft light brown sugar
finely grated zest of 1 small orange

1 cup ready-to-eat dried apricots, chopped
1 cup sweetened dried cranberries
2 eggs, beaten
⅔ cup milk

1 Remove the kneading blade from the bread pan. Remove the bread pan from the machine, grease and line the bottom and sides of the pan, and set aside.

2 Sift the flour and baking powder into a bowl, then lightly cut in the butter. Stir in the sugar, orange zest, and dried fruit. Add the eggs and milk and mix together until thoroughly combined. Spoon the batter into the bread pan and smooth the surface.

3 Place the bread pan in position in the machine and close the lid. Set the machine to "Bake Only" for 60 minutes. Press Start.

4 After baking, a fine skewer inserted into the middle of the loaf should come out clean. If the loaf requires more baking, bake on the same setting 10 to 15 minutes longer, or until baked through.

5 Remove the bread pan from the machine using oven mitts, then leave to stand 5 minutes, before turning the loaf out onto a wire rack to cool. Serve warm or cold in slices.

Acknowledgments

My special thanks go to my husband, Robbie, for his continued support and encouragement with this book and for his tireless tasting of many of the recipes. My sincere thanks also go to Sarah Bradford and Bev Saunder for all their dedicated hard work testing recipes, and to Gwen Whiting for her help with typing recipes. The publishers would like to thank Allison Furbish and Joan Dunn of King Arthur Flour.